*W*ildflowers of **Cape Cod**

and the Islands

Over 200 Wildflowers that Grow
on Cape Cod's Sand Dunes,
Heathlands, Pond Shores,
Woodlands, Bogs, and Meadows

Kate Carter

The Countryman Press
Woodstock, Vermont

We welcome your comments and suggestions.
Please contact Editor, The Countryman Press,
P.O. Box 748, Woodstock, VT 05091,
or e-mail countrymanpress@wwnorton.com.

ISBN 978-0-88150-791-1

Book design and composition by the author.
Photography by the author unless otherwise
noted.

Published by The Countryman Press,
P.O. Box 748, Woodstock, VT 05091

Distributed by W. W. Norton & Company, Inc.,
500 Fifth Avenue, New York, NY 10110

Printed in China

10 9 8 7 6 5 4 3 2 1

Contents

The Flowers

Front cover (left to right): Starflower, frostweed, Virginia meadow beauty, trumpet creeper, stout blue-eyed grass. **Back cover:** Blue curls, Plymouth gentian, spotted wintergreen, sickle-leaf golden aster.

Acknowledgments

Many knowledgeable people on Cape Cod helped me with this book, and I am grateful for their interest and generosity. I'd especially like to thank Dennis Murley of the Wellfleet Bay Wildlife Sanctuary for taking the time to meet with me, give me a tour of the Center's trails, and direct me to other places where I would find many wildflowers to photograph. It was also a pleasure to meet botanist Mario J. DiGregorio, who shared his vast knowledge of the Cape's wildflower community and also graciously lent me several photos to include in this book. Don Schall of the Cape Cod Botany Club helped me find several plants and provided me with a source to confirm the recent changes in plant nomenclature. Jessie M. Harris is a prolific plant photographer, and she provided several photos of flowers I didn't find.

I'd also like to thank several friends who kept me company during my Cape outings: Nicki Houghton, who could spot a wildflower a mile away; Carla Hesler, for finding the Wellfleet cabin; Deborah Coleman, who provided moral support when my camera fell into West Reservoir; my sister Joanne Woodward, who blocked the wind; Caro Thompson, who loaned me her tent and cat-sat while I was gone; and my best buddies Brewster and Phoebe, who sat patiently and watched me take every photo I shot for this book.

Photo Info

All photographs by Kate Carter were taken with a 35mm digital Canon D60 or D30 with a 50mm macro lens, or occasionally with a 28-105 zoom lens. Photos were processed in Photoshop and the book's layout was done on PageMaker for PC.

Introduction

Cape Cod has hundreds of wildflowers, including native species and exotic ones that escaped to the wild from gardens or were brought to this country in other products. This guidebook features 206 wildflowers, both native and exotic, that can easily be seen on the Cape's sand dunes, heathlands, pond shores, woodlands, bogs, and meadows. Some flowers are in full view beside roads we travel every day. Others you must venture into the woods to find, and still others you can only see by walking the beaches and dunes or paddling around a pond.

This guidebook includes the Cape's most common wildflowers, including herbaceous flowers, which die back to the ground every year, and woody shrubs and vines, which put out new growth every year from old stems and branches. Most of the Cape's endangered flowers, those flowers that are in immediate danger of becoming extirpated, are not included here since it is unlikely you will see them.

Because a flower's most obvious attribute is its color, the flowers in this book are arranged by color. Within each color section they are arranged alphabetically by family, then by genus and species. See pages ix to xvi for more information on the families included in this guide.

Size is also an important characteristic. Some flowers are as big as plates and others so small you'll have to get down on your hands and knees to see them. The flower's size is indicated in the text description (Flower), as is the plant's height (Plant).

In the descriptions, common names appear first, with alternative names in parentheses. The scientific names are below the common names, with family names to the right. Because the scientific nomenclature has changed in recent years, I have listed the new scientific name first, with the old name below it in parentheses. Then follows a brief description of each flower's noteworthy features. At the end of the description I have noted if the plant is a native species (Native) or, if not, where it is from (Europe, Eurasia, etc.). Below that are flower size, plant height, blooming time, habitat, and dates and locations of the photographs (if available).

Where to Go

It's remarkable how many flowers you will see if you know where to look. Roadside flowers are easy; they line Cape Cod's roads all summer long. To see flowers whose habitats are woods, bogs, streambanks, pond shores, and sand dunes, I recommend visiting these locations:

Wellfleet Bay Wildlife Sanctuary, just off Route 6, S. Wellfleet. The sanctuary has a wide range of flowers in bloom, common and rare, from April through October. The sanctuary became one of my favorite places to visit on the Cape, and I came here often to take photos for this book. Admission is $5 for adults and free to members of the Massachusetts Audubon Society.

Ashumet Holly Wildlife Sanctuary, Ashumet Road, N. Falmouth. The main attractions here are Grassy Pond and the 65 varieties of holly trees. Many woodland flowers can be found on the walking trails in the spring, and a diverse collection of common and unusual wildflowers grow around Grassy Pond during July and August. Admission is $3 for adults and free to members of the Massachusetts Audubon Society.

Harwich conservation lands, off Bells Neck Road, W. Harwich. This area has a diverse ecosystem, with wooded walking trails, riverbanks, pond shores, and cranberry bogs, all in the vicinity of West Reservoir and Herring River.

Cape Cod Museum of Natural History, Route 6A, Brewster. The trails on this property take walkers to riverbanks, woodlands, salt marshes, and sand dunes. My favorite is the John Wing Trail, which takes you from the parking lot to Cape Cod Bay.

Province Lands Visitor Center, Province-town. Here you will find wooded walking trails, open fields, dunes, a beech forests, and a bike path. The area supports a diverse habitat, including native and exotic species.

References

I found the following books useful during my research:

Walking the Cape and Islands, by David Weintraub, 2006, Menasha Ridge Press.

The Flora of Cape Cod, by Hanry K. Svenson and Robert W. Pyle, 1979, The Cape Cod Museum of Natural History.

Wildflowers of Cape Cod, by Harold R. Hinds and Wilfred A. Hathaway, 1968, The Chatham Press.

Cape Cod Wildflowers: A Vanishing Heritage, by Mario J. DiGregorio and Jeff Wallner, 1989, Mountain Press Publishing; 2003, University Press of New England.

Cape Cod Street Atlas, 2005, Arrow Map, Inc.
—**Kate Carter**

Flower Families

Specific characteristics appear in all the flowers that belong to the same family. Here is a list of the families included in this book and their most distinctive features.

Arum, *Araceae*—A large hoodlike leaf (spathe) surrounds, and often hides, a columnar spike (spadix) crowded with tiny flowers.

Aster, *Asteraceae*—The "flower" is actually many flowers on a receptacle; small fertile nonshowy "disk" flowers are surrounded by larger sterile petal-like "ray" flowers, as in a daisy. Many variations. A large flower family.

Balsam, *Balsaminaceae*—Irregularly-shaped dangling flowers. Stems translucent and watery, leaves thin. Ripe pods spring open when touched, ejecting seeds.

Bellflower, *Campanulaceae*—Bell-shaped flowers with 5 flaring fused petals, 5 stamens, 1 pistil. Two subfamilies: Bluebell *(Campanuloideae)* and Lobelia *(Lobelioideae)*.

Bignonia, *Bignoniaceae*—Flowering plants comprised mainly of trees, shrubs, and a few herbaceous plants. Distributed mostly in the tropics and subtropics, but with a number of temperate species as well.

Bladderwort, *Lentibulariaceae*—Rootless carnivorous plants of wet areas. Lipped flowers emerge above water on leafless stems; leaves filamentous, underwater.

Borage, *Boraginaceae*—Flowers on ends of stems that uncurl with growth.

Broomrape, *Orobanchaceae*—Parasitic plants without green color and with only scalelike leaves. Flowers have 4 or 5 partly united sepals and 4 or 5 united petals.

Buckbean, *Menyanthaceae*—Aquatic and wetland plants with simple or compound leaves that arise alternately from a creeping rhizome.

Buttercup, *Ranunculaceae*—Large family whose flowers have many stamens and pistils forming a button or bushy central cluster. Sometimes petals absent, sepals showy.

Cactus, *Cactaceae*—Succulent plants native to the Americas that are adapted to extremely arid and hot environments, showing a wide range of features that conserve water.

Cashew, *Anacardiaceae*—Trees, shrubs, and vines with resinous sap. Leaves usually alternate. Flowers small, in panicles, often honey scented, usually regular, hermaphrodite, fruits mostly drupes.

Clethra, *Clethraceae*—Flowering plants native to tropical regions of Asia and the Americas.

Crowberry, *Empetraceae*—Dwarf evergreen shrubs that bear edible berrylike fruit, commonly found in the Northern Hemisphere from temperate to subarctic climates. Typical habitat is moorlands, tundra, and muskeg, but also spruce forests.

Evening-Primrose, *Onagraceae*—Most with showy flowers, flower parts in 4s. Stigma like a cross. Flowers usually open in evening or morning, close in afternoon.

Figwort, *Scrophulariaceae*—Swollen tube flowers have odd-shaped "mouth" with 2 lips. Blossoms arranged in spires.

Gentian, *Gentianaceae*—Flowers with several fused petals (4 or more) and one stamen attached to each. Leaves usually opposite or whorled, stemless.

Geranium, *Geraniaceae*—Flower, usually pink or lavender, with parts in 5s. After petals fall, pistil shows as a long spike, the "crane's bill." Leaves usually alternate, divided.

Ginseng, *Araliaceae*—Tiny 5-part flowers in puffy clusters, like starbursts. Leaves highly divided into big leaflets. Fruit fleshy, with stony seeds.

Heath, *Ericaceae*—Mostly woody shrubs, some creeping herbs. Petals fused into hanging bells. Simple, often thick leaves. Species here occur mostly in acid soils, bogs, and pine barrens.

Indian Pipe, *Monotropaceae*—Small waxy-looking plants without chlorophyll.

Iris, *Iridaceae*—Plants with swordlike leaves and showy flowers with parts in 3s (petals, sepals, stamens, styles).

Leadwort, *Plumbaginaceae*—Mostly perennial herbaceous plants; a few woody shrubs. All have symmetric flowers pollinated by insects and are found in many different climatic regions, from arctic to tropical, but are especially associated with salt marshes.

Lily, *Liliaceae*—Perennials from bulbs, leaves with parallel veins. Flowers shaped like bells, triangles or stars, with parts in 3s or multiples of 3.

Lobelia, *Lobelioideae*—See Bellflower Family.

Loosestrife, Lythraceae—Slender herbs with purple flowers having 3 to 6 petals. Flowers in leaf axils or in spikes.

Madder, *Rubiaceae*— Tiny flowers with parts of 4. Leaves in pairs or whorls. Bedstraws are creeping plants, with square stems and small leaves in whorls.

Mallow, *Malvaceae*—Showy flowers with 5 big petals and 5 sepals. Stamens encircle the protruding style, the whole becoming a distinctive column.

Mangosteen, *Clusiaceae*—Clusters of mostly yellow flowers with 5 petals, bushy clump of stamens at the center. Leaves paired, untoothed, with dark or translucent dots or glands.

Melastome, *Melastomataceae*—3 to 9 major leaf veins run in a parallel fashion from the base of the blade to near the leaf tip. The leaves are usually opposite.

Milkweed, *Asclepiadaceae*—Plants have milky juice. Flowers grouped in domes, star-shaped with 5 swept-back petals and an unusual 5-part center. Leaves usually opposite. Fruit a large, long pod containing seeds with long silky fibers.

Mint, *Lamiaceae*—Tiny flowers in spikes or clusters at leaf joints. Petals fused into a tube with two lobed "lips." Leaves usually scented and opposite, stems usually square.

Morning Glory, *Convolvulaceae*—Herbaceous trailing vines with funnel-shaped flowers, each with 5 stamens. Stems often have a milky juice. Leaves alternate and simple, heartshaped in many.

Mustard, *Brassicaceae*—Has 4 petals, wide at ends, narrow at centers, that make a cross. Distinctive seed pod.

Nightshade, *Solanaceae*—Flower parts in 5s. Stamens and pistil make a prominent beak. Fruit a pod or berry.

Orchid, *Orchidaceae*—Flowers irregular, with 3 sepals, 2 lateral petals, and a third larger petal forming a pouch, balloon, or lip. Leaves toothless, smooth, parallel veined.

Orpine (Stonecrop), *Crassulaceae*—These plants store their water in succulent leaves, and often grow in dry places.

Parsley (Carrot), *Apiaceae*—Many tiny 5-petaled flowers clustered in flat tops or umbrella-shaped heads. Leaves usually lacy. Many are poisonous.

Pea, *Fabaceae*—Irregular flowers with 5 petals: a larger top banner, 2 side wings, and 2 that unite at the bottom into a "keel." Leaves usually compound. Seeds are in distinctively shaped, 2-valved pods, often edible.

Pink, *Caryophyllaceae*—5 notched petals spreading flat from a sac-like center. Opposite leaves at swollen joints.

Pipewort, *Eriocaulaceae*—Mostly herbaceous perennial plants, a few annuals, with small, wind-pollinated flowers. They tend to be associated with wet soils, many growing in shallow water.

Pitcher Plant, *Sarraceniaceae*—Carnivorous bog plants with tubular leaves at the base that hold water in which insects drown. 5-petaled, 5-sepaled single flowers on separate stalks, stigma shaped like a huge parasol.

Pokeweed, *Phytolaccaceae*—Contains phytolaccatoxin and phytolaccigenin, which are poisonous to mammals, but not to birds. Leaves alternate, pointed at ends, with crinkled edges. Stems often pink or red. Flowers greenish white, in long clusters at ends of stems, becoming dark purple berries.

Poppy, *Papaveraceae*—Poppy subfamily *(Papaveroideae)* has opaque or colored sap, showy flowers in multiples of 4, and lobed leaves. Bleeding Heart subfamily *(Fumarioideae)* has flowers hanging in a row from same side of stem, leaves finely cut.

Primrose, *Primulaceae*—One stamen at the center of each of 5 petals. Leaves simple, usually opposite or whorled.

Rock-Rose, *Cistaceae*—Low shrubs and some herbaceous plants that prefer dry, sunny habitats, often having showy yellow, pink, or white flowers, which are generally short lived. They grow well in poor soil and many are cultivated in gardens.

Rose, *Rosaceae*—5 roundish petals, 5 sepals, stamens in a circle around the center of the flower.

Smartweed (Buckwheat), *Polygonaceae*—Swollen joints where alternate leaves attach to stem. No petals, but small, petal-like sepals, usually clustered at ends of stems.

Spurge, *Euphorbiaceae*—A large, mostly tropical family. Leaves are usually alternate and are mainly simple, occasionally palmate. Flowers are radially symmetric, with the male and the female flowers usually occurring on the same plant.

Sundew, *Droseraceae*—Carnivorous bog plants. Leaves, rising from the base, have hairs tipped with sticky droplets that snare insects. Small flowers bloom along a leafless stem.

Vervain, *Verbenaceae*—Mintlike small flowers form slender, pencil-like spikes or flat clusters at tops of plant. Leaves paired, toothed.

Violet, *Violaceae*—Low plants with irregular flowers: 5 petals, the lowest often wider, heavily veined, and extending back to a spur; the 2 side petals usually bearded. Pistil thick and short.

Spiderwort, *Commelinaceae*—Succulent herbs, mostly perennials, from the tropics. Petals are so thin they only last a day.

Water-Hyacinth, *Pontederiaceae*—Aquatic plants of marshes and slow-moving waters. Dark glossy leaves, erect or floating. 6-petaled flowers, often arranged in spikes.

Water-Lily, *Nymphaeaceae*—Aquatic plants rooted in the mud, with leaves floating on the surface. Large, showy flowers on separate stalks.

Water-Plantain, *Alismataceae*—Aquatic plants whose flowers, on leafless stems, have 3 petals (usually white) and 3 sepals.

Wintergreen, *Pyrolaceae*—Flowers with parts in 5s, usually hanging down and shaped like little umbrellas. Leaves usually evergreen.

Wood Sorrel, *Oxalidaceae*—Heart-shaped cloverlike leaves with 3 leaflets. Flower parts in 5s.

Dusty Miller (Beach Wormwood)

Artemisia stelleriana　　　　*Aster*

Tiny yellowish flowers in leafy stiff spikes. Leaves deeply lobed, white-woolly on both sides. Often cultivated for its foliage, escaped to beaches and dunes. Eurasia.

Flower: Under ¼ inch.
Plant: 12–30 inches.
Blooming: May–September.
Habitat: Beaches and dunes.
Photo: June 11, Province Lands Visitor Center, Provincetown.

1

Swamp Beggar's Ticks (Stick-Tight)

Bidens connata   *Aster*

Small erect yellowish brown flower heads
on long stems. Flowers never fully open.
Leaves opposite, narrow, toothed, stemmed.
Fruit has 2–4 barbs that stick to clothing.
Native.

Flower: 1 inch. **Plant:** 1–4 feet.
Blooming: August–October.
Habitat: Wet places.
Photo: August 27, Harwich conservation
land trails, West Reservoir, W. Harwich.

Yellow Thistle

Cirsium horridulum   *Aster*

This thistle has nearly disappeared on
the mainland, but is fairly common
on Nantucket. Leaves alternate, deeply
divided, sharp toothed. Leaves and stem
prickly. Native.

Flower: 3 inches.
Plant: 1–3 feet.
Blooming: June–July.
Habitat: Coastal sandy fields, salt marsh
edges.
Photo: Courtesy Mario J. DiGregorio.

Long-Stalked Tickseed (Coreopsis)

Coreopsis lanceolata   *Aster*

Flowers with 6–10 bright yellow rays
toothed at ends. Leaves opposite, entire,
long, lance shaped. Escaped from
cultivation in Northeast. Native.

Flower: 1½–2½ inches.
Plant: 10–24 inches.
Blooming: June–August.
Habitat: Dry sandy soil, roadsides, fields.
Photo: June 11, Province Lands Visitor
Center, Provincetown.

Slender Fragrant Goldenrod
Euthamia tenuifolia
(Solidago tenuifolia)   *Aster*

Tiny yellow flowers form flat-topped clusters at top of plant. Leaves alternate, entire, smooth, narrow, grass like. Similar to sweet goldenrod (page 13), but leaves narrower. Native.

Flower: ¼ inch. **Plant:** 1–2 feet.
Blooming: July–October.
Habitat: Dry sandy soil, open woods, fields.
Photo: August 7, Ashumet Holly Wildlife Sanctuary, W. Falmouth.

Mouse-Ear Hawkweed
Hieracium pilosella
(Pilosella officinarum)   *Aster*

Dandelion like flower, usually 2–4 heads, sometimes just one. Leaves basal, entire. Stem and leaves hairy. Europe.

Flower: ½–1 inch.
Plant: 4–30 inches.
Blooming: May–September.
Habitat: Disturbed areas.
Photo: June 9, Lowell Holly Reservation walking trails, Mashpee.

Rattlesnake Weed

Hieracium venosum   *Aster*

Dandelionlike flower, numerous heads, stem smooth with few to no leaves. Basal leaves entire, dark green, with dark red veins. Native.

Flower: 1 inch.
Plant: 6–30 inches.
Blooming: May–July.
Habitat: Dry woods and clearings, fields.
Photo: June 11, Nickerson State Park, Little Cliff Pond Trail, Brewster.

Sickle-Leaf Golden Aster
Pityopsis falcata
(Chrysopsis falcata)   *Aster*

Mat-forming plant with bright yellow
flowers. Stems densely lined with furry,
gray-green, bladelike leaves. Native.
Flower: 1 inch.
Plant: 8–15 inches.
Blooming: July–September.
Habitat: Dry sandy soil near coast, pine
barrens.
Photo: July 22, John Wing Trail, Cape
Cod Museum of Natural History,
Brewster.

Black-Eyed Susan

Rudbeckia hirta   *Aster*

Abundant and showy standout with long bloom season. Yellow petals surround dark brown protruding disk. Stem and leaves coarse and hairy, leaves alternate. Makes a good cutting flower. Native.

Flower: 2–3 inches.
Plant: 1–3 feet
Blooming: June–October.
Habitat: Disturbed areas.
Photo: July 23, Long Point Wildlife Refuge, Martha's Vineyard.

Canada Goldenrod
Solidago canadensis
(S. altissima)   *Aster*

Tiny flowers on top side of numerous
branches form graceful plumes. Stems
grayish, slightly downy. Leaves long, narrow,
slightly toothed, alternate; topsides rough,
undersides downy. Native.
Flower: ¼ inch (plumes 3–5 inches).
Plant: 2–5 feet. **Blooming:** July–October.
Habitat: Moist or dry open places.
Photo: August 28, Ashumet Holly
Wildlife Sanctuary, W. Falmouth.

Early Goldenrod

Solidago juncea   *Aster*

Numerous tiny yellow flowers line top
sides of branching stems, forming dense,
arcing plumes. One of the first goldenrods
to bloom. Leaves alternate, entire, bladelike;
tiny leaflets grow where bigger leaves
attach to stem. Native.

Flower: ¼ inch (plumes 4 inches).
Plant: 1–4 feet. **Blooming:** July–September.
Habitat: Open woods, roadsides, dry soil.
Photo: July 23, Long Point Wildlife
Refuge, Martha's Vineyard.

Gray Goldenrod

Solidago nemoralis   *Aster*

Tiny yellow flowers grow in plume-shaped clusters on one side of stem. Leaves alternate, obscurely toothed. Leaves and stem grayish, finely hairy. Native.

Flower: ¼ inch (plumes up to 5 inches).
Plant: 1–3 feet.
Blooming: July–October.
Habitat: Sandy soils, dry woods, open places.
Photo: August 28, Ashumet Holly Wildlife Sanctuary, W. Falmouth.

Sweet Goldenrod

Solidago odora   *Aster*

Tiny flowers form plumes at ends of stems. Leaves alternate, entire, lanceshaped, pointed at both ends, smooth, with obvious parallel veins. Similar to slender fragrant goldenrod (page 5), but leaves not as narrow. Native.

Flower: ¼ inch (plumes 3–4 inches).
Plant: 2–3 feet. **Blooming:** July–September.
Habitat: Open woods, dry soil.
Photo: September 9, Province Lands Visitor Center, Provincetown.

Downy Goldenrod
Solidago puberula   *Aster*

Tiny flowers grow in clusters, forming
long, slender rods. Leaves alternate,
lanceshaped, pointed at both ends, lower
ones toothed. Native.

Flower: ½ inch.

Plant: 1–3 feet.

Blooming: August–October.

Habitat: Dry open woods, sandy areas.

Photo: September 13, Nickerson State
Park, Brewster.

Rough-Stemmed Goldenrod (Wrinkle-Leaved Goldenrod)

Solidago rugosa   *Aster*

Stiff, slightly bristly stems and fuzzy toothed leaves distinguish this goldenrod from other plumed goldenrods. Also, its plumes branch out more symmetrically, less one-sided. Native.

Flower: ¼ inch (plumes 4–6 inches).
Plant: 1–7 feet.
Blooming: July–October.
Habitat: Various habitats.
Photo: Stock photo.

Seaside Goldenrod

Solidago sempervirens   *Aster*

Flowers larger than all other goldenrod
flowers, each with 8–10 rays. Leaves
alternate, entire, smooth, somewhat waxy,
an adaptation to salty air. Native.
Flower: ¼–½ inch (plumes 3–6 inches).
Plant: 1–7 feet.
Blooming: August–November.
Habitat: Salt marshes.
Photo: September 23, Crowe's Pasture,
East Dennis.

Bog Goldenrod (Swamp Goldenrod)

Solidago uliginosa   *Aster*

Flowers form wandlike plumes. Stems smooth, leaves smooth, alternate, tapered at both ends, finely toothed. Native.

Flower: ¼ inch (plumes 2–4 inches).
Plant: 2–5 feet.
Blooming: August–September.
Habitat: Bogs, swamps, pond shores.
Photo: August 29, Four Ponds Conservation Area, Bourne.

Humped Bladderwort
Utricularia gibba
(U. biflora)   *Bladderwort*

Carnivorous plant with submerged root
system; stalks rise straight up out of the
water. Flowers two-lipped, with lips
nearly equal in size, growing singularly or
clustered. No leaves. Native.

Flower: ½ inch. **Plant:** 3–5 inches.
Blooming: July–August.
Habitat: Wet shores and bogs.
Photo: August 27, Harwich conservation
land trails, West Reservoir, W. Harwich.

Creeping Buttercup

Ranunculus repens   ***Buttercup***

Shiny yellow 5-petaled flowers on erect stems. Leaves deeply divided into 3 sections, long stemmed. Entire plant somewhat hairy. Europe.

Flower: ½ inch.
Plant: 6–12 inches.
Blooming: May–July.
Habitat: Roadsides, moist meadows, open areas.
Photo: May 23, Shawme-Crowell State Forest walking trails, Sandwich.

Prickly Pear Cactus

Opuntia humifusa   *Cactus*

Sprawling cactus armed with thorny
bristles. Big swollen joints; large showy
yellow flowers. Classified as Endangered
on the "Massachusetts List of Endangered,
Threatened, and Special Concern Species."
Native.

Flower: 2–3 inches. **Plant:** 6–18 inches.
Blooming: June–August.
Habitat: Sandy fields, dunes, lower Cape.
Photo: June 24, Wellfleet Bay Wildlife
Sanctuary, S. Wellfleet.

Common Evening-Primrose

Oenothera   *Evening-*
biennis   *Primrose*

Tall leafy stalk with many yellow 4-petaled flowers on long stems. Leaves long, narrow, alternate. Flowers open fully at night. Native.

Flower: 1–1½ inches.
Plant: 1–5 feet.
Blooming: June–September.
Habitat: Dry open places.
Photo: July 10, Wellfleet Bay Wildlife Sanctuary, S. Wellfleet.

Fern-Leaf False Foxglove
Aureolaria pedicularia
(Gerardia pedicularia)   Figwort

Yellow funnel-shaped flowers with 5 petals, downy on outsides. Bushy plant with sticky, hairy stems, deeply cut fernlike opposite leaves. Smooth yellow false foxglove *(A. flava)* has smooth stems, leaves entire, similar flowers. Native.

Flower: 1–1½ inches. **Plant:** 1–4 feet.
Blooming: July–September.
Habitat: Dry woods.
Photo: September 11, Wellfleet roadside.

Golden Hedge-Hyssop (Golden Pert)

Gratiola aurea   *Figwort*

Tubular-shaped yellow flowers with 4 petals. Leaves small, paired. Low creeping plant. Native.

Flower: ½ inch.

Plant: 3–12 inches.

Blooming: June–September.

Habitat: Sandy shores and swamps.

Photo: August 7, Ryder Conservation Area, Mashpee.

Butter and Eggs

Linaria vulgaris *Figwort*

Two-toned yellow and orange irregularly
shaped flowers with spurs, growing in
racemes. Flowers resemble the familiar
garden snapdragon. Leaves numerous,
alternate, very narrow. Europe.

Flower: ½–1 inch.
Plant: 1–3 feet.
Blooming: July–September.
Habitat: Roadsides, dry fields, bare lawns.
Photo: August 29, the Knob, Falmouth.

Common Mullein

Verbascum thapsus   *Figwort*

Many 5-petaled flowers are packed together to form dense, clublike spikes. Leaves alternate, entire, velvety, numerous. Europe.

Flower: 1 inch.
Plant: 2–6 feet.
Blooming: June–September.
Habitat: Roadsides, fields, open areas.
Photo: Stock photo.

Yellow Flag

Iris pseudacorus **Iris**

An obvious iris, similar to blue flag (page 152), but nonnative and highly invasive. It came to the U.S. from Europe and escaped cultivation.

Flower: 2–3½ inches.
Plant: 2–4 feet.
Blooming: May–July.
Habit: Marshes, wet areas.
Photo: Stock photo.

Trout Lily (Dogtooth Violet)

Erythronium americanum　　　　*Lily*

Single flower with 6 yellow curled-back petals on leafless stems. 2 basal leaves are green, mottled with brown, resembling trout bellies. Native.

Flower: 1½–2 inches.
Plant: 4–8 inches.
Blooming: April–May.
Habitat: Rich woods.
Photo: May 8, Murkwood Forest, Sandwich.

Yellow Stargrass (Common Goldstar)

Hypoxis hirsute   *Lily*

Tiny 5-petaled flowers at ends of numerous branches. Small scalelike leaves grow in sparse pairs. Native.

Flower: ¼ inch.
Plant: 3–10 inches.
Blooming: July–September.
Habitat: Sterile, sandy soil.
Photo: July 23, Tisbury Meadow Preserve, Martha's Vineyard.

Sessile Bellwort (Wild Oats)
Uvularia sessilifolia   *Lily*
Single dangling flower with 6 buttery
yellow petals forming elongated bell shape.
Leaves alternate, oblong, pointed at ends,
entire. Stem forked above middle. Native.
Flower: 1 inch.
Plant: 6–18 inches.
Blooming: April–June.
Habitat: Woods.
Photo: May 23, Shawme-Crowell State
Forest walking trails, Sandwich.

Orange-Grass

Hypericum gentianoides   ***Mangosteen***

Yellow flowers with 6 petals, flowers loosely clustered at top of stem. Grasslike leaves 4–6 inches tall at bloom time, growing to 12 inches after flower dies. Native.

Flower: ¾ inch.

Plant: up to 1 foot.

Blooming: May–September.

Habitat: Meadows and open woods.

Photo: May 22, Moraine Trails near Goodwill Park, Falmouth.

Common St. John's-Wort

Hypericum perforatum   Mangosteen
Bushy branching plant with many 5-
petaled dark yellow flowers. Petals have
black dots on margins. Many prominent
stamens. Small opposite leaves. Common.
Europe.
Flower: 1 inch.
Plant: 1–2½ feet.
Blooming: June–September.
Habitat: Fields, meadows, roadsides.
Photo: June 24, Wellfleet Bay Wildlife
Sanctuary, S. Wellfleet.

Common Winter Cress

Barbarea vulgaris *Mustard*

Common and familiar plant with 4-petaled yellow flowers tightly clustered at ends of upright stalks. Leaves resemble arugula or other salad greens. Eurasia.

Flower: 1 inch.
Plant: 1–2 feet.
Blooming: May–September.
Habitat: Disturbed areas, fields, lawns, roadsides.
Photo: June 14, Indian Neck town beach, Wellfleet.

Black Mustard

Brassica nigra   *Mustard*

4-petaled flowers line stalk's upper half.
Brown upright pea pods hug stems.
Widely branching plant. Often considered
a weed. Europe.

Flower: ½–¾ inches.
Plant: 2–4 feet.
Blooming: June–October.
Habitat: Disturbed areas, roadsides, lawns.
Photo: May 22, Moraine Trails near
Goodwill Park, Falmouth.

Mossy Stonecrop

Sedum acre   *Orpine*

Bright yellow flowers with 5, sometimes 4, pointed petals. Matted fleshy plant. Leaves small, alternate, entire, overlapping, thick, fleshy. Escaped from cultivation. Europe.

Flower: ½ inch.

Plant: 1–3 inches.

Blooming: June–August.

Habitat: Rocky dry banks, roadsides.

Photo: June 12, Wellfleet roadside.

Wild Indigo

Baptisia tinctoria   *Pea*

Multibranching plant with yellow pealike
flowers in racemes at ends of long stems.
Leaves usually 3 leaflets, entire, small,
broad, blunt at tip. Native.

Flower: ½ inch.

Plant: 1–3 feet.

Blooming: July–August.

Habitat: Sandy dry areas, sterile fields.

Photo: July 23, Tisbury Meadow Preserve,
Martha's Vineyard.

Partridge Pea
Chamaecrista fasciculata
(Cassia fasciculata)   *Pea*
Yellow flowers growing on long stems
from leaf axils; 5 petals, 10 stamens (4 with
yellow anthers, 6 with purple). Leaflets
entire, growing in 6–15 pairs. Europe.
Flower: 1 inch.
Plant: Climbing 1–3 feet.
Blooming: July–September.
Habitat: Sandy soil.
Photo: September 13, Province Lands
Visitor Center, Provincetown.

Scotch Broom

Cytisus scoparius **Pea**

Stiffly branched shrub with yellow pea-shaped flowers near ends of branches. Leaflets entire, in 3s near base of plant, reducing to single leaf higher up. Flowers turn to flat brown pea pods. Europe.

Flower: 1 inch. **Plant:** 3–5 feet.

Blooming: May–June.

Habitat: Disturbed areas, sandy soil along coast.

Photo: June 11, Province Lands Visitor Center, Provincetown.

Birdfoot Trefoil

Lotus corniculatus   *Pea*

Bright yellow irregularly shaped flowers in
terminal clusters. Cloverlike leaves in 3s,
plus 2 at base of leaf stem. Europe.

Flower: ½ inch.
Plant: 6–18 inches.
Blooming: June–September.
Habitat: Roadsides, cleared areas.
Photo: August 7, Ashumet Holly Wildlife
Sanctuary, W. Falmouth.

Hop Clover

Trifolium aureum
(T. agrarium)   *Pea*

Low plant with dense flower clusters.
Puffy petals form small heads at ends of
short stems. Flowers fade to brown with
age and resemble the fruit of common
hops (page 60). Europe.
Flower: ½ inch.
Plant: 6–12 inches.
Blooming: June–August.
Habitat: Roadsides, fields, lawns.
Photo: June 13, Wellfleet roadside.

Celandine

Chelidonium majus   *Poppy*

Leafy plant with hairy stems and deep
yellow 4-petaled flowers in loose clusters.
Leaves bluish green. Plant has saffron-
colored juice that's poisonous to chickens.
Europe.

Flower: ¾ inch.
Plant: 1–3 feet.
Blooming: May–July.
Habitat: Wood edges.
Photo: June 12, Salt Pond Visitor Center,
Eastham.

Whorled Loosestrife

Lysimachia quadrifolia   *Primrose*

Yellow star-shaped flowers on long stems.
Flowers have 5 petals, each with red
dots at center forming circular pattern.
4 flowers and 4 leaves join stem at same
place, forming whorles. Fast-spreading by
underground stems. Native.

Flower: 1 inch.
Plant: 2–3 feet.
Blooming: June.
Habitat: Open woods, thickets.
Photo: June 25, the Knob, Falmouth.

Yellow Loosestrife (Swamp Candles)

Lysimachia terrestris   *Primrose*

Dense spike of many star-shaped flowers, with circles of red spots at centers. Flowers have long stems. Petals arch back. Leaves opposite, long, slender. Native.

Flower: 1 inch. **Plant:** 2–3 feet.

Blooming: June–August.

Habitat: Swampy areas, grassy shores, wet thickets.

Photo: July 9, Harwich conservation land trails, West Reservoir, W. Harwich.

Frostweed

Helianthemum   *Rock-*
canadense   *Rose*

Bright yellow flowers with 5 wedge-
shaped petals. Flowers last only one day.
Leaves small, alternate, lanceshaped, pale
beneath. Native.

Flower: 1 inch.
Plant: 1 foot.
Blooming: June–August.
Habitat: Sand barrens and dry areas.
Photo: June 12, Wellfleet roadside.

Beach Heather (Poverty Grass)

Hudsonia   *Rock-*
tomentosa   *Rose*

Plants form large mounds. Bright 5-petaled star-shaped flowers at ends of scaly stems. Tiny woolly leaves hug stems. Plant covered with grayish white hairs. Native.

Flower: ¼ inch.

Plant: 1–2 feet.

Blooming: May–June.

Habitat: Heathlands and dunes.

Photo: June 10, Marconi Beach, Wellfleet.

Old-Field Cinquefoil
(Dwarf Cinquefoil)

Potentilla canadensis   *Rose*

Trailing plant with small pale yellow 5-petaled flowers on long stems. Sepals green, pointed, obvious. Leaves toothed, with 5 leaflets. Spreads by runners. Native.

Flower: Under 1 inch. **Plant:** 6 inches.

Blooming: May–June.

Habitat: Dry woods and fields, disturbed areas.

Photo: May 7, Indian Lands Conservation Area, Dennis.

Rough-Fruited Cinquefoil (Sulphur Cinquefoil)

Potentilla recta   *Rose*

Loose cluster of pale yellow 5-petaled flowers on erect bushy plant. Petals slightly indented at ends. Narrow leaves, fuzzy on underside. Common. Europe.

Flower: 1 inch.
Plant: 1–2 feet.
Blooming: June–August.
Habitat: Fields, roadsides, pastures.
Photo: June 11, Province Lands Visitor Center, Provincetown.

Common Cinquefoil

Potentilla simplex   *Rose*

Cinquefoil is French for "five-fingered" and refers to the plant's leaf arrangement of five, dark green, sharply toothed leaflets. Weak-stemmed trailing plant with 5-petaled flowers on long stems. Sepals green, pointed, obvious. Native.
Flower: ½–¾ inch. **Plant:** 6–20 inches.
Blooming: April–June.
Habitat: Dry fields, open woods.
Photo: May 21, Lowell Holly Reservation walking trails, Mashpee.

Cypress-Spurge
Euphorbia cyparissias   *Spurge*
Densely tufted low-growing plant. Tiny
yellowish green flowers clustered in
erect umbels at top of stem. Flowers turn
reddish with age. Leaves entire, alternate,
narrow, light green. Eurasia.
Flower: 2–inch clusters.
Plant: 6–12 inches.
Blooming: May–September.
Habitat: Open areas, roadsides.
Photo: June 12, Wellfleet roadside.

Yellow Pond Lily
(Bullhead Lily, Spadderdock)
Nuphar lutea
(N. variegatum)   *Water-Lily*

Aquatic yellow flower with large heart-shaped leaves that float on water's surface. Odd, cup-shaped flowers never completely open. Native.

Flower: 2 inches. **Plant:** 4–8 inches.
Blooming: June–September.
Habitat: Ponds, slow-moving water.
Photo: June 25, Beebe Woods pond, Falmouth.

Yellow Wood Sorrel

Oxalis stricta *Wood Sorrel*

Small yellow 5-petaled flowers on branching stems with whitish hairs. Leaves have 3 heart-shaped leaflets, similar to clover leaflets. Common. Native.

Flower: ½ inch.
Plant: 3–15 inches.
Blooming: May–August.
Habitat: Roadsides, fields, lawns.
Photo: July 10, Wellfleet Bay Wildlife Sanctuary, S. Wellfleet.

Use this inch ruler to
measure flower size
and plant height.

1 —

—

2 —

—

3 —

—

4 —

—

5 —

—

6 —

Rose Pogonia, see page 196.

51

Jack-in-the-Pulpit

Arisaema triphyllum   *Arum*

Green and purple striped hooded tube
(spathe) growing beneath a large 3-part
leaf. Within the tube is Jack (spadix), like a
preacher in his pulpit. Spadix covered with
minuscule flowers that become bright red
berries in August. Native.

Flower: minuscule, spadix 2–4 inches.
Plant: 1–3 feet.
Blooming: April–June.
Habitat: Wet rich woods.
Photo: Stock photo.

Skunk Cabbage

Symplocarpus foetidus   *Arum*

Tiny white flowers packed tightly in a ball (spadix) are hidden within the brownish green mottled hood (spathe). Flower appears in early spring, followed later by huge dark green leaves that have a skunky odor when crushed. Native.

Flower: Minuscule, spadix 1–3 inches.
Plant: 2–5 inches.
Blooming: Late March–May.
Habitat: Rich wet woods, soils, swamps.
Photo: April 26, Green Briar Nature Center, Sandwich.

Pilewort (Fireweed)

Erechtites hieraciifolia   *Aster*

Greenish white flowers, swollen at the
base, with a brush like tip. Flowers do not
open. Hairy stem, leaves lance shaped,
alternate, deeply toothed, coarse. Native.
Flower: ½–¾ inches.
Plant: 1–7 feet.
Blooming: July–October.
Habitat: Clearings and thickets, often on
recently burned land.
Photo: September 10, Wellfleet Bay
Wildlife Sanctuary, S. Wellfleet.

Beach Clotbur

Xanthium echinatum   *Aster*

Greenish flowers of two types: upper staminate flowers in short spikes; lower pistillate flowers form burrs ½–¾ inch long, growing in leaf axils. Leaves long stalked, broad, coarsely toothed or lobed; stem purple blotched. Eurasia.

Flower: ½–¾ inches. **Plant:** 1–3 feet.
Blooming: July–October.
Habitat: Disturbed or sandy areas.
Photo: September 14, John Wing Trail, Cape Cod Museum of Natural History, Brewster.

Beechdrops

Epifagus virginiana   *Broomrape*

Parasitic plant that feeds off beech tree roots. Irregularly shaped reddish brown tubular flowers. Scaly stem, no leaves. Native.

Flower: ½ inch.
Plant: 6–20 inches.
Blooming: August–October.
Habitat: Beech woods.
Photo: September 13, Province Lands Beech Forest Trail, Provincetown.

Curly Dock

Rumex crispus **Buckwheat**

Unattractive plant with stout stalks
from which dangle tiny greenish yellow,
sometimes reddish, flowers. Big leaves have
wavy, or curled, edges. Native.

Flower: ¼ inch.
Plant: 1–4 feet.
Blooming: June–September.
Habitat: Fields, roadsides, open areas.
Photo: June 25, the Knob, Falmouth.

Common Poison-Ivy

Toxicodendron radicans *Cashew*

Tiny whitish yellowish greenish flowers
with 5 petals growing in clusters from leaf
axils. Leaves in 3s, shiny, alternate, long
stemmed, turning red with age. Berries a
dull yellowish-white.

Plant: Shrubs 1–4 feet; vines up to 20 feet.
Blooming: May–June.
Habitat: Wooded areas, streambanks,
thickets, clearings, beach dunes, yards.
Photos: Throughout Cape Cod.
Notes: Poison-ivy is prevelant and
pervasive on the Cape, thriving in many

habitats. The poison in poison-ivy is a resinlike oil called urushiol (oo-roo-she-all). It only takes one nanogram (billionth of a gram) to cause a rash, though the average is 100 nanograms for most people. One-quarter of an ounce is all that is needed to cause a rash in every person on earth. Urushiol oil will stay active on any surface, including dead plants, for up to five years. Contact with the oil causes the rash, whether it's on a plant, clothing, bedding, or a pet, or by rubbing it from one part of your body to another. You spread the rash only if urushiol oil is present. Native.

Common Hops

Humulus lupulus **Hemp**

Climbing vine with no tendrils. Flowers small, 5-petaled, greenish white, growing in loose axillary clusters. Leaves toothed, deeply lobed, with 3–5 lobes. Fruit a drooping cluster of brown, overlapping brachs. Used to make beer. Europe.
Flower: ¼ inch. **Plant:** Climbing 3–6 feet.
Blooming: July–September.
Habitat: Thickets, dry open areas.
Photo: August 7, Ashumet Holly Wildlife Sanctuary, W. Falmouth.

Indian Cucumber Root

Medeola virginiana   *Lily*

Hard-to-see yellowish green flowers
dangle under one set of whorled leaves at
top of tall stalk. Another set of whorled
leaves halfway down stalk. Native.

Flower: 1–1½ inches.
Plant: 1–3 feet.
Blooming: May–June.
Habitat: Rich woods.
Photo: June 25, Murkwood Forest,
Sandwich.

Hairy Solomon's Seal

Polygonatum pubescens   *Lily*

Small bell-shaped greenish yellow flowers
dangle in pairs from leaf axils. Leaves
alternate, oval, with obvious parallel veins,
slightly hairy beneath. Native.

Flower: ¼ inch (3–4 inch plumes).
Plant: 1–3 feet.
Blooming: May–June.
Habitat: Rich woods.
Photo: Stock photo.

Helliborine

Epipactus helleborine   *Orchid*

Odd-shaped whitish brown flowers in racemes on single stalks. Leaves alternate, entire, with noticeable parallel veins. Lower leaves much broader than upper ones. Europe.

Flower: ½–¾ inches.

Plant: 12–18 inches.

Blooming: July–September.

Habitat: Roadsides, woods.

Photo: July 9, Harwich conservation land trails, West Reservoir, W. Harwich.

Yarrow

Achillea millefolium   *Aster*

Tiny 5-petaled flowers in tight clusters
form flat tops. Leaves gray-green,
intricately cut, fernlike, alternate. Does
well in wildflower gardens. Native.

Flower: ¼ inch (clusters 1–3 inches).
Plant: 1–3 feet.
Blooming: June–August.
Habitat: Dry open areas, roadsides, fields.
Photo: June 11, Province Lands Visitor
Center, Provincetown.

Pearly Everlasting

Anaphalis margaritacea   Aster

Pearly white pea size flowers form clusters at ends of stems. Flowers open slightly, revealing yellow centers. Plant is nonbranching, with fuzzy alternate narrow leaves. A great choice for dried flower arrangements. Native.

Flower: ¼ inch. **Plant:** 1–3 feet.
Blooming: July–September.
Habitat: Disturbed areas, dry soils, open woods.
Photo: Stock photo.

Plantain-Leaved Pussytoes

Antennaria plantaginifolia   *Aster*

Clusters of tiny whitish flowers on single stems. Stems and leaves downy. Bottom leaves larger, rounder; upper leaves small, sparse, lance shaped. The Cape has several pussytoes, difficult to distinguish. This is the most common. Native.

Flower: ½-inch clusters. **Plant:** 4–9 inches.
Blooming: April–June.
Habitat: Disturbed, dry areas.
Photo: April 24, Thompson's Field, Harwich.

Daisy Fleabane

Erigeron annuus   *Aster*

Small white to slightly pink flowers
with numerous stubby fringelike rays
surrounding yellow disks. Plant has
many branches, fuzzy stems and leaves.
Extremely common, considered a weed by
some. Native.

Flower: ½–¾ inches. **Plant:** 1–4 feet.
Blooming: June–September.
Habitat: Open areas, roadsides.
Photo: June 14, Indian Neck town beach,
Wellfleet.

Hyssop-Leaved Thoroughwort

Eupatorium hyssopifolium　　*Aster*

White flowers with numerous rays form flat-topped clusters on branching plant. Leaves narrow, slightly toothed, in whorls of 3 or 4, with clusters of smaller leaves growing in axils. Native.

Flower: ¼ inch (clusters 1–3 inches).
Plant: 1–3 feet.
Blooming: July–September.
Habitat: Dry sandy fields.
Photo: July 23, Tisbury Meadow Preserve, Martha's Vineyard.

Boneset

Eupatorium perfoliatum   *Aster*

Clusters of tiny white flowers atop many branching stems, making for a wide, flat-topped appearance. Stems hairy; leaves opposite, textured, hairy, clasping, appearing joined at the base. Native.

Flower: ¼ inch (clusters 2–5 inches).
Plant: 2–4 feet.
Blooming: July–September.
Habitat: Moist open areas.
Photo: August 7, Ashumet Holly Wildlife Sanctuary, W. Falmouth.

White Wood Aster

Eurybia divaricata
(Aster divaricatus)   ***Aster***

White narrow rays surround a yellow disk.
Disk turns brown with age. Leaves heart
shaped, toothed, alternate, longstemmed.
Native.

Flower: ¾–1 inch.
Plant: 1–3 feet.
Blooming: August–October.
Habitat: Dry woods and clearings.
Photo: September 13, Nickerson State
Park, Brewster.

Ox-Eye Daisy

Leucanthemum vulgare
(Chrysanthemum
leucanthemum) **Aster**

Common and familiar plant with large
showy flowers atop single erect stalks.
Many white rays surround a yellow disk,
whose center is slightly depressed. This is
the classic roadside daisy. Native.

Flower: 1–2 inches. **Plant:** 1–3 feet.
Blooming: June–August.
Habitat: Fields, roadsides, pastures.
Photo: June 12, Salt Pond Visitor Center,
Eastham.

Fragrant Everlasting (Catfoot)

*Pseudognaphalium obtusifolium
(Gnaphalium obtusifolium)*   *Aster*

Small flower heads in branching clusters.
Leaves alternate, narrow, bladelike.
Fragrant, common, abundant. Native.
Flower: ¼ inch. **Plant:** 1–2 feet.
Blooming: August–October.
Habitat: Open disturbed areas, dry fields,
woods margins.
Photo: September 9, Province Lands
Visitor Center, Provincetown.

Toothed Whitetop Aster

Sericocarpus asteroides
(Aster paternus)   *Aster*

An aster whose rays you can count.
Usually there are 5, sometimes 4, forming
flat-topped clusters. Leaves narrow,
alternate, entire. Native.

Flower: ½ inch.
Plant: 12–18 inches.
Blooming: July–September.
Habitat: Dry woods.
Photo: July 23, Tisbury Meadow Preserve,
Martha's Vineyard.

Silverrod

Solidago bicolor   *Aster*

Cape Cod's only white goldenrod. Tiny, pale white flowers are crowded along upper half of long cylindrical spikes. Stems gray and hairy. Leaves alternate, entire, tapering to tips. Native.

Flower: ¼ inch.
Plant: 1–3 feet.
Blooming: July–October.
Habitat: Dry open woods and fields.
Photo: September 13, Nickerson State Park, Brewster.

Heath Aster

Symphyotrichum ericoides
(Aster ericoides)　　　　*Aster*

White or pinkish ray flowers surround a
yellow disk. Erect dense-looking stiff plant.
Small, narrow, alternate, stiff, heathlike
leaves. Native.

Flower: ½ inch.
Plant: 1–3 feet.
Blooming: August–October.
Habitat: Dry open sites, disturbed areas.
Photo: August 29, the Knob, Falmouth.

Perennial Salt-Marsh Aster

Symphyotrichum tenuifolius
(Aster tenuifolius)   *Aster*

Erect plant with minimal branching.
Flowers white or pale lilac. Leaves few,
alternate, long, narrow, fleshy. Native.
Flower: ½–1 inch.
Plant: 12–18 inches.
Blooming: August–October.
Habitat: Salt marshes.
Photo: September 10, Wellfleet Bay
Wildlife Sanctuary, S. Wellfleet.

Little Floating Heart

Nymphoides cordata   *Buckbean*

Aquatic plant with small 5-petaled white
flowers and distinctly yellow centers. Plant
grows from submerged tubers. Leaves
heart shaped, long stalked, floating on
surface. Native.

Flower: ½ inch.

Plant: Just above water.

Blooming: June–September.

Habitat: Ponds, slow-moving water.

Photo: Courtesy Mario J. DiGregorio.

Sand Jointweed

Polygonella articulate   *Buckwheat*

Tiny white (sometimes pink) flowers with 5 petals growing in racemes. Stem wiry and jointed, leaves threadlike, unobtrusive. Native.

Flower: ¼ inch.

Plant: 4–10 inches.

Blooming: August–October.

Habitat: Dry acidic sands, salt marshes.

Photo: September 12, Wellfleet Bay Wildlife Sanctuary, S. Wellfleet.

Japanese Knotwood (Mexican Bamboo)

Polygonum cuspidatum   *Buckwheat*

Large bushlike plant with broad pointed leaves, jointed stems. Tiny white flowers grow in branching sprays from leaf axils. Highly invasive; grows in dense stands that crowd out native plant and animal habitat. Europe.

Flower: ¼ inch (sprays 4–6 inches).

Plant: 4–10 feet.

Blooming: July–October.

Habitat: Waste places, roadsides, open areas, streambanks.

Photo: September 10, Eastham roadside.

Wood Anemone (Windflower)

Anemone quinquefolia   **Buttercup**

Delicate woodland flower often forms
sizeable stands. Flowers single, with short
stems and 5 white to pinkish or pale bluish
petals. Leaves long stemmed, in 3s, whorled,
each divided into 5 leaflets. Native.
Flower: 1 inch. **Plant:** 4–8 inches.
Blooming: Late April–June.
Habitat: Moist woods.
Photo: May 8, Murkwood Forest,
Sandwich.

Clematis (Virgin's Bower)

Clematis virginiana   *Buttercup*

Climbing woody vine. Flowers with
4 bright white sepals, no petals, bushy
central stamen cluster. 3 coarsely toothed
leaflets, rounded to slightly heart shaped at
base, smooth on both sides. Native.

Flower: 1 inch.

Plant: Climbing 10–20 feet.

Blooming: July–September.

Habitat: Streambanks, borders of swamps,
woods, thickets.

Photo: September 11, Truro Center
roadside.

Sweet Pepper-Bush

Clethra alnifolia   *Clethra*

Potent, sweetly scented shrub. Tiny
white 5-petaled flowers in long racemes.
Protruding style. Leaves alternate, egg
shaped, upper half sharply toothed.
Native.

Flower: ½ inch (racemes 2–3 inches).
Plant: 3–8 feet. **Blooming:** August.
Habitat: Swamps and moist woods near
the coast.
Photo: August 6, Wellfleet Bay Wildlife
Sanctuary, S. Wellfleet.

Turtlehead

Chelone glabra   *Figwort*

Appropriately named, the tubular 2-lipped flowers resemble turtle heads. White or pale pink flowers clustered at tops of stems. Leaves opposite, toothed, long, narrow. *Chelone* means tortoise. Native.

Flower: 1–1½ inches.

Plant: 1–3 feet.

Blooming: July–September.

Habitat: Streambanks, pond edges.

Photo: August 29, Four Ponds Conservation Area, Bourne.

Cow-Wheat

Melampyrum lineare   *Figwort*

Tiny whitish flowers with yellow lower lips, growing in pairs in leaf axils. Lower leaves lance shaped, entire. Upper leaves small, slightly toothed. Native.

Flower: ½ inch.
Plant: 4–12 inches.
Blooming: June–August.
Habitat: Rich woods.
Photo: June 11, Little Cliff Pond Trail, Nickerson State Park, Brewster.

Bristly Sarsaparilla

Aralia hispida   *Ginseng*

Golf ball size flower clusters at tops of
erect, bristly stems. Flowers and leaves on
same stems. 3 to 5 sharply toothed leaflets.
Fruit is a cluster of dark blue berries.
Native.

Flower: 1–1½ inch clusters.
Plant: 1–3 feet.
Blooming: June–July.
Habitat: Rich woods.
Photo: June 24, Shankpainter Pond
conservation area, Provincetown.

Wild Sarsaparilla
Aralia nudicaulis   *Ginseng*

Tiny whitish green flowers form golf ball size clusters on long erect leafless stems. Each plant usually has 3-4 of these arrangements. Leaves on separate stalks with 3 branches, each branch having 5 leaflets. Native.

Flower: ¼ inch (clusters 1½ inches).
Plant: 6–15 inches. **Blooming:** May–June.
Habitat: Rich dry woods.
Photo: May 21, Lowell Holly Reservation walking trails, Mashpee.

Bearberry (Hog Cranberry)

Arctostaphylos uva-ursi   *Heath*

Bell-shaped white to pale pink flowers
with red stems in end clusters. Leaves
alternate, entire, shiny above, paler beneath.
Fruit a small red berry. Native.

Flower: Under ½ inch.

Plant: Up to 1 foot.

Blooming: May–June.

Habitat: Coastal sands and dunes, open
sandy areas.

Photo: May 7, Thompson's Field,
Harwich.

Trailing Arbutus

Epigaea repens **Heath**

Early spring creeping evergreen plant with 5-petaled white or pale pink flowers; slightly hairy pale yellow centers. Several flowers at ends of hairy trailing stems. Leaves broad, oval, leathery looking, pale beneath. Native. **Flower:** ½ inch. **Plant:** Creeping 3–6 inches.

Blooming: April–May.

Habitat: Sandy or rocky woods.

Photo: April 23, Little Cliff Pond Trail, Nickerson State Park, Brewster.

Wintergreen
(Teaberry, Checkerberry)

Gaultheria procumbens   *Heath*

Tiny waxy bell-shaped flowers dangle beneath thick shiny oval leaves. Plants often form small stands. Flowers become dry red berries. Native.

Flower: ¼ inch. **Plant:** 3–6 inches.

Blooming: July–August.

Habitat: Woods, clearings, especially coniferous/mixed woods and acidic soils.

Photo: July 23, Tisbury Meadow Preserve, Martha's Vineyard.

Black Huckleberry

Gaylussacia baccata   *Heath*

Common shrub, with flowers narrowly
bell-shaped, red-tinged, growing in one-
sided clusters. Leaves bluntly pointed at
both ends, yellowish green, resin dots on
underside. Flowers become small, nearly
black berries. Native.

Flower: ¼ inch. **Plant:** 2–3 feet.
Blooming: May–June.
Habitat: Sandy dry woods and thickets.
Photo: May 23, Shawme-Crowell State
Forest walking trails, Sandwich.

Common Lowbush Blueberry

Vaccinium angustifolium   *Heath*

Common shrub with white or pink-tinged bell-shaped flowers hanging in clusters. Leaves alternate, entire, smooth on both sides, paler beneath. Native.
Flower: ¼–½ inch. **Plant:** 1–3 feet.
Blooming: May–June.
Habitat: Dry sandy or rocky woods and clearings.
Photo: May 23, Shawme-Crowell State Forest walking trails, Sandwich.

Japanese Honeysuckle

Lonicera japonica   *Honeysuckle*

Climbing vine with white flowers in pairs,
turning yellow with age, very fragrant.
Flowers become black berries. This
invasive plant can smother out other plants
with its rank growth. Asia.

Flower: 1–1½ inches.
Plant: Climbing to 12 feet.
Blooming: June–August.
Habitat: Disturbed open sandy areas,
roadsides.
Photo: June 24, Nauset Light, Eastham.

Indian Pipe

Monotropa uniflora   *Indian Pipe*

A plant with no chlorophyll, so it doesn't photosynthesize; nutrients come from decaying matter. Whitish waxy scaly stalks; nodding waxy bell-shaped flowers. Solo or in clumps. Pinesap *(M. hypopithys)* looks similar, but flowers in terminal clusters, yellowish, turning reddish in fall. Native.

Flower: 1 inch. **Plant:** 4–10 inches.
Blooming: July–September.
Habitat: Rich woods.
Photo: July 9, Cape Cod Rail Trail, Brewster.

Canada Mayflower

Maianthemum canadense   *Lily*

Small woodland plant with tiny 4-petaled flowers clustered on stems like miniature bottle brushes. 2–3 large bright shiny clasping leaves. Often forms large colonies. Native.

Flower: Under ¼ inch (clusters 2 inches).
Plant: 3–6 inches.
Blooming: May–June.
Habitat: Rich woods and clearings.
Photo: May 21, Lowell Holly Reservation walking trails, Mashpee.

Starry Solomon's Plume (Starry False Solomon's Seal)

Maianthemum stellatum
(Smilacina stellata)   *Lily*

Tiny white flowers with 6 petals growing in terminal racemes. Leaves smooth, alternate, entire, clasping. Native.

Flower: ¼ inch.
Plant: 1–2 feet.
Blooming: May–August.
Habitat: Moist sandy woods.
Photo: Courtesy Jessie M. Harris.

Yucca

Yucca filamentosa   ***Lily***

Nodding white flowers with 6 petals form
large round blooms that grow on panicles
several feet long. Leaves basal, large, thick,
entire, rigid. Native to Virginia and south,
cultivated and escaped locally.

Flower: 1½–2 inches.
Plant: 5–10 feet.
Blooming: July–September.
Habitat: Old fields, roadsides.
Photo: July 9, Brewster roadside.

Northern Bedstraw

Galium boreale   *Madder*

Abundant weedy looking plant comprised of tiny 4-petaled white flowers at ends of many scrawny branches. Thin leaves in whorls of 4 on stem and branches. Supports itself by leaning on other plants. Native.

Flowers: ¼ inch. **Plant:** 1–3 feet.
Blooming: June–August.
Habitat: Open woods, moist areas, rocky shores.
Photo: Stock photo.

Partridgeberry

Mitchella repens   *Madder*

Creeping plant with one pair of 4-petaled flowers at end of stem. Petals hairy, stamens protruding. Leaves opposite, small, round, shiny. Flowers turn to bright red berries in fall. Native.

Flower: ½–¾ inch.
Plant: 1–3 inches.
Blooming: June–July.
Habitat: Woods.
Photo: Stock photo.

Northern Bugleweed

Lycopus uniflorus   *Mint*

Tiny white flowers grow in whorls in leaf
axils. Leaves opposite, toothed, smooth.
Square smooth stem. Native.

Flower: Under ¼ inch.
Plant: 12–24 inches.
Blooming: July–September.
Habitat: Wet soils.
Photo: August 28, Ashumet Holly
Wildlife Sanctuary, W. Falmouth.

Hedge Bindweed
Calystegia sepium
(Convolvulus sepium)   *Morning Glory*

Vine with showy funnel-shaped flowers, usually white, sometimes pale pink or pale lavender. Leaves triangular arrow shaped, alternate, entire. Native.

Flower: 1½–3 inches.
Plant: Climbing to 12 feet.
Blooming: July–September.
Habitat: Open disturbed areas, dry fields.
Photo: June 24, Nauset Light, Eastham.

Bushy-Branched Sea Rocket

Cakile edentula   *Mustard*

Small inconspicuous 4-petaled white or lavender flowers. Leaves alternate, wavy toothed, thick and fleshy. Native.

Flower: ¼–½ inch.

Plant: 6–12 inches.

Blooming: July–September.

Habitat: Coastal sands and dunes, above high-tide line.

Photo: August 29, the Knob, Falmouth.

Watercress

Rorippa nasturtium-aquaticum
(Nasturtium officinale)　　*Mustard*

Tiny white flowers with 4 petals. Leaves
divided into 4–9 nearly entire, nearly
round leaflets. Roots submerged in mud
or water. Europe.

Flower: ¼ inch.
Plant: 4–10 inches.
Blooming: July–September.
Habitat: Ponds, slow-moving water.
Photo: September 8, Four Ponds
Conservation Area, Bourne.

Jimson-Weed (Thorn-Apple)

Datura stramonium   *Nightshade*

Large white to pale pink or pale lavender
funnel-shaped flowers with 5 flaring
petals. Leaves alternate, egg shaped, coarsely
toothed, sharply pointed at ends. Fruit a
spiny 2-inch pod. Poisonous. Europe.

Flower: 1–4 inches.
Plant: Climbing 1–5 feet.
Blooming: June–August.
Habitat: Waste areas.
Photo: Courtesy Jessie M. Harris.

Nodding Ladies' Tresses

Spiranthes cernua   *Orchid*

Fragrant irregularly shaped white flowers
spiral up single spikes. Flowers nod slightly.
Leaves long, narrow, entire, rising from
base. Native.

Flower: ½ inch.

Plant: 6–20 inches.

Blooming: August–October.

Habitat: Moist woods, swamps, sandy
places.

Photo: September 11, High Head sand
dunes, N. Truro.

Queen Anne's Lace

Daucus carota   *Parsley*

Many tiny flowers form lacy flat-topped heads. Bristly stems, finely cut fernlike leaves. Also called bird's nest for its late-summer look (after flowering, in seed). Common. Europe.

Flower: ¼ inch (clusters 2–4 inches).
Plant: 2–4 feet.
Blooming: July–September.
Habitat: Roadsides, open areas.
Photo: July 9, Harwich conservation land trails, West Reservoir, W. Harwich.

Umbellate Water-Pennywort

Hydrocotyle umbellate　　　　*Parsley*

Tiny greenish white flowers form small round clusters on top of long slender stems. Leaves round, with scalloped edges on very long stems. Roots submerged. Native.

Flower: Under ¼ inch (1-inch ball).
Plant: 3–6 inches.
Blooming: July–September.
Habitat: Pond areas.
Photo: September 13, Gull Pond, Wellfleet.

White Sweet Clover

Melilotus alba   *Pea*

Tall bushy plant with flowers spread out on long slender spikes. Leaves in 3s. Used by farmers in plant rotation to add nitrogen and other nutrients to soil. Sweet odor when mowed. Europe.

Flower: ¼–½ inch (spikes 2–6 inches).
Plant: 3–8 feet.
Blooming: May–August.
Habitat: Roadsides, field edges.
Photo: July 9, Harwich conservation land trails, West Reservoir, W. Harwich.

Mouse-Ear Chickweed

Cerastium fontanum
(C. vulgatum)   *Pink*

Tiny white flowers, mostly at ends of
branching stems. Flowers have 5 deeply
notched petals, 5 prominent sepals. Leaves
opposite, small, slightly hairy. Europe.
Flower: ½ inch. **Plant:** 6-12 inches.
Blooming: May–September.
Habitat: Common weed of gardens,
roadsides, lawns.
Photo: May 22, Moraine Trails near
Goodwill Park, Falmouth.

White Campion
(Evening Lychnis)

Silene latifolia
(Lychnis alba, S. alba)   *Pink*

White to pinkish flowers open at night
and on overcast days. 5 petals so deeply
notched they look like 10. Petals fold out
at ends of veiny sacks. Hairy branching
stem; hairy opposite leaves. Europe.
Flower: 1–1½ inches. **Plant:** 1–2½ feet.
Blooming: June–August.
Habitat: Roadsides, fields, open areas.
Photo: June 10, Marconi Beach, Wellfleet.

Common Pipewort

Eriocaulon aquaticum   ***Pipewort***

White flowers in buttonlike heads atop
single slender stems. Grasslike basal leaves
are often partially submerged. Native.

Flower: ½-inch heads.

Plant: 2–10 inches.

Blooming: July–September.

Habitat: Pond edges.

Photo: September 13, Gull Pond,
Wellfleet.

Pokeweed

Phytolacca americana   *Pokeweed*

Distinctive stout succulent plant. Flowers
in racemes, with 5 white to pinkish round
waxy sepals (not petals), green centers.
Leaves large, egg shaped, alternate, entire.
Stems turning red with age, berries dark
blue. Native.

Flower: ¼ inch (racemes 3–6 inches).
Plant: 4–10 feet. **Blooming:** July–September.
Habitat: Open woods, fields, fencerows.
Photo: July 10, Wellfleet Bay Wildlife
Sanctuary, S. Wellfleet.

Starflower

Trientalis borealis   *Primrose*

2 delicate flowers (sometimes only 1) on
slender stems above whorl of shiny leaves.
Each flower has 5–9 (usually 6–7) pointed
petals and 7 long stamens. Leaves often
different sizes, in whorls. Native.

Flower: ½–¾ inches.

Plant: 4–9 inches.

Blooming: May–June.

Habitat: Cool dry woods.

Photo: May 21, Lowell Holly Reservation
walking trails, Mashpee.

Common Strawberry (Wild Strawberry)

Fragaria virginiana   ***Rose***

Miniature version of cultivated strawberries. Small 5-petaled flowers on upright stems. Sharply toothed leaves in 3s on separate stems. Abundant. Spreads by runners. Produces sweet berries. Native.
Flower: ½ inch. **Plant:** 3–6 inches.
Blooming: April–June.
Habitat: Sunny fields, open areas.
Photo: June 9, Lowell Holly Reservation walking trails, Mashpee.

Beach Plum

Prunus maritime   ***Rose***

Early blooming shrub with white flowers
in small clusters growing along branches.
5 rounded petals, many stamens. Leaves
clustered, toothed, pointed at ends. Native.
Flower: 1 inch.
Plant: 1–8 feet.
Blooming: April–May.
Habitat: Dunes, roadsides.
Photo: Courtesy Mario J. DiGregorio.

Multiflora Rose

Rosa multiflora *Rose*

White 5-petaled flowers in long-stemmed
clusters. Compound leaves with 7–9
toothed leaflets; stems sparsely thorned.
Hips are small, round, dull red. Europe.
Flower: 1 inch.
Plant: 2–12 feet.
Blooming: June–July.
Habitat: Old farms, pastures, roadsides.
Photo: June 12, Salt Pond Visitor Center,
Eastham.

Dewberry

Rubus flagelleris   *Rose*

Blackberry-like plant, but low and trailing. Leaflets in 3s. Small showy flowers, with five petals; stamens a bushy cluster. Leaves sharply notched, stems prickly. Native.

Flower: 1 inch.

Plant: 4–12 inches.

Blooming: June–July.

Habitat: Woods, borders, dry fields, clearings, thickets.

Photo: June 9, Lowell Holly Reservation walking trail, Mashpee.

Meadowsweet

Spiraea alba (S. latifolia) **Rose**

Shrub with white, occasionally pinkish flowers with 5 petals in branching, spike-like terminal clusters; long prominent stamens. Leaves alternate, toothed, downy beneath. Native.

Flower: ¼ inch (spikes 3–6 inches).
Plant: 2–6 feet. **Blooming:** July–September.
Habitat: Damp open places, old fields and pastures, swamps, streambanks.
Photo: August 7, Ashumet Holly Wildlife Sanctuary, W. Falmouth.

117

Arrow-Leaved Tearthumb

Polygonum sagittatum   *Smartweed*

Tiny white or pale pink dense flower clusters on ends of thin weak branching stems. Leaves alternate, narrow, arrow shaped. Leaves and stems sticky/prickly. Native.

Flower: Under ¼ inch (¾-inch clusters).
Plant: 2–4 feet.
Blooming: June–October.
Habitat: Low thickets, wet open places.
Photo: Stock photo.

Strap-Leaved Violet
(Lance-Leaved) Violet

Viola lanceolata   *Violet*

Typical-looking white violet, but leaves
lance shaped, not heart shaped. Flowers
and leaves on separate stems. Leaves wavy
edged to slightly toothed. Native.

Flower: ½ inch.
Plant: 2–6 inches.
Blooming: April–June.
Habitat: Bogs, damp meadows, shores.
Photo: Courtesy Jessie M. Harris.

Wild White Violet (Pale Violet)

Viola macloskeyi (V. pallens)   Violet

Common violet with 5 petals, the lower one purple veined. Leaves rounded, scalloped edges, heart shaped at base. Leaves and flowers grow on separate stems. Native.

Flower: ½ inch.

Plant: 2–5 inches.

Blooming: April–June.

Habitat: Dry or moist woods, clearings.

Photo: Courtesy Jessie M. Harris.

Fragrant Water-Lily

Nymphaea odorata   *Water–Lily*

Beautiful aquatic flower with numerous white petals and yellow centers. Huge round leaves float on water's surface. Lovely floral odor. Native.

Flower: 3–5 inches.

Plant: 3–6 inches above water.

Blooming: July–September.

Habitat: Ponds, slow-moving water.

Photo: August 29, Four Ponds Conservation Area, Bourne.

Broadleaf Arrowhead (Common Arrowhead)

Sagittaria latifolia   ***Water-Plantain***

Long arrow-shaped leaves. Separate stems
have white flowers, each with 3 broad petals,
yellow centers. Ducks eat its tuberous roots.
Slender arrowhead *(S. teres)* has smaller
flowers, narrow cylindrical basal leaves;
grows along coast. Native.

Flower: 1 inch. **Plant:** 1-3 feet.

Blooming: July–September.

Habitat: Shallow fresh water.

Photo: August 27, Harwich conservation
land trails, West Reservoir, W. Harwich.

Spotted Wintergreen

Chimaphila maculate   Wintergreen

Erect plant with evergreen leaves and reddish stems. Flowers waxy white, with 5 recurved petals, pronounced stamens and pistil. Leaves in whorls, widely toothed, with white stripe down center vein. Red stems. Pipsissiwa *(C. umbellata)* is similar, but leaves are solid green. Native.

Flower: 1 inch. **Plant:** 4–10 inches.
Blooming: July–August.
Habitat: Woods.
Photo: July 9, Cape Cod Rail Trail, Brewster.

Jewelweed (Spotted Touch-Me-Not)

Impatiens capensis   *Balsam*

Tubular spotted orange flowers dangle like
pendants from branch ends of leafy plant.
Spur curls under flower. Leaves alternate,
egg shaped, toothed. Stems watery,
translucent. Native.

Flower: 1 inch. **Plant:** 3–5 feet.

Blooming: July–September.

Habitat: Wet ground, shady places.

Photo: August 6, Harwich conservation
land trails, West Reservoir, W. Harwich.

Trumpet-Creeper

Campsis radicans   *Bignonia*

Woody vine with bright reddish orange tubular-shaped 5-petaled flowers. 7–11 opposite leaflets. Long-stemmed leaflets toothed, pointed at ends. Native.

Flower: 2 inches.
Plant: Climbing to 12 feet.
Blooming: July–September.
Habitat: Banks, woods, roadsides.
Photo: August 6, Fort Hill parking lot, Eastham.

Wild Columbine

Aquilegia canadensis   *Buttercup*

Bright red flowers with 5 spurred petals
and long protruding yellow stamens.
Leaflets in 3s, deeply lobed. A favorite of
hummingbirds. Native.

Flower: 1–1½ inches.
Plant: 1–3 feet.
Blooming: April–June.
Habitat: Rich rocky woods.
Photo: Stock photo.

Broom-Crowberry

Corema conradii   *Crowberry*

Low evergreen shrub forms large mounds.
Tiny reddish brown flowers cluster at tips of
branches. Leaves small, bright green. needle
like. Fruit is pin-head sized, dark brown.
Listed as Special Concern on the "Massa-
chusetts list of Endangered, Threatened, and
Special Concern Species." Native.
Flower: Under ¼ inch. **Plant:** 5–10 inches.
Blooming: March–April.
Habitat: Heathlands, dunes, sandy shores.
Photo: April 24, Wellfleet Bay Wildlife
Sanctuary, S. Wellfleet.

Wood Lily
Lilium philadelphicum   *Lily*

Erect orange 6-petaled flowers on a
stiff stalk. Leaves in whorls, large, entire,
pointed. A striking flower that is becoming
less common on the Cape. Native.

Flower: 2 inches.
Plant: 1–3 feet.
Blooming: June–August.
Habitat: Dry woods, thickets, sandy soils.
Photo: Courtesy Mario J. DiGregorio.

Turk's-Cap Lily

Lilium superbum   *Lily*

Orange flowers dangle from long stems; 6 recurved petals; prominent stamens; yellow "star" in flower's center distinguishes it from the common roadside tiger lily, a garden escapee from Europe. Native.

Flower: 2–3 inches.
Plant: 3–7 feet.
Blooming: July–September.
Habitat: Wet meadows, open areas.
Photo: Courtesy Mario J. DiGregorio.

Cardinal Flower

Lobelia cardinalis   *Lobelia*

Can't be mistaken for any other wildflower. Red, slightly tubular flowers, with 5 flaring petals and prominent pistil on tall slender spikes. Leaves long, narrow, alternate, toothed. Native.

Flower: 1–1½ inches.
Plant: 2–4 feet.
Blooming: July–August.
Habitat: Streambanks, wet areas.
Photo: August 6, Harwich conservation land trails, West Reservoir, W. Harwich.

Butterfly-Weed

Asclepias tuberose   *Milkweed*

Showy orange flowers with recurved petals grow in umbels. Leaves narrow, entire, alternate. Stems hairy. A favorite of monarch butterflies. Native.

Flower: ½ inch (clusters 3–5 inches).
Plant: 1–2 feet.
Blooming: June–August.
Habitat: Upland woods, sandy soils.
Photo: July 9, Thompson's Field, W. Harwich.

Common Groundnut

Apios americana **Pea**

Irregularly shaped brownish red flowers in compact round clusters, growing on long stems from leaf axils. 5–7 broad tapering leaflets. Native.

Flower: ½ inch.
Plant: Trailing up to 4 feet.
Blooming: July–August.
Habitat: Freshwater marshes, meadows, thickets.
Photo: Stock photo.

Northern Pitcher-Plant

Sarracenia purpurea   *Pitcher–Plant*

Odd-looking carnivorous plant with one reddish brown nodding terminal flower on a leafless stalk. At bases of plants are tube like purple-veined leaves shaped like narrow pitchers. These water-filled tubes trap and drown insects, providing the plant with nitrogen. Native.

Flower: 1½–2 inches. **Plant:** 8–24 inches.
Blooming: June–August.
Habitat: Bogs and fens.
Photo: Stock photo.

Scarlet Pimpernel
(Poor Man's Weatherglass)

Anagallis arvensis   *Primrose*

Red-orange flowers with 5 petals and
a central purple circle. Flowers on long
stems, growing from paired leaf axils.
Leaves opposite, entire, stemless. Sprawling,
weedy plant. Eurasia.

Flower: ¼ inch.
Plant: 2–6 inches.
Blooming: June–September.
Habitat: Salted highways, sandy soil.
Photo: Courtesy Jessie M. Harris.

Spotted Knapweed
Centaurea biebersteinii
(C. maculosa)   *Aster*

Long-lasting lavender to pinkish flowers in thistle like heads. Plant is multi-branching, with numerous flower heads. Leaves sparse, divided into narrow segments. Considered invasive in some states. Europe.

Flower: 1-inch heads. **Plant:** 1–3 feet.
Blooming: July–August.
Habitat: Roadsides, disturbed areas.
Photo: July 22, visitor center parking lot, Sandwich.

Chicory

Cichorium intybus   *Aster*

Chicory's intense blue color sets it apart from all other roadside flowers. Stiff stalk has numerous stemless flower heads whose petals are fringed at ends. Each flower lasts only a day. The coffee substitute/additive comes from this plant's roots. Europe.

Flower: 1–1½ inches. **Plant:** 2–4 feet.
Blooming: June–October.
Habitat: Roadsides, waste areas.
Photo: July 23, Tisbury Meadow Preserve, Martha's Vineyard.

Field Thistle

Cirsium discolor   *Aster*

Well-armed plant with purple flower
heads on erect stems. Leaves alternate,
deeply cut, extremely spiny. Small upper
leaves embrace flower head. Native.

Flower: 2 inches.
Plant: 3–7 feet.
Blooming: July–October.
Habitat: Fields, open areas, roadsides.
Photo: September 22, Crane Wildlife
Management Area, Falmouth.

Low Showy Aster
Eurybia spectabilis
(Aster spectabilis)   *Aster*

Bright violet rays surround a yellow
disk. Leaves narrowly egg shaped, entire,
alternate; leaves near base are long
stemmed. Native.

Flower: 1–1½ inches.
Plant: 1–2 feet.
Blooming: August–October.
Habitat: Dry sandy soil and pine barrens.
Photo: September 22, Crane Wildlife
Management Area, Falmouth.

Stiff Aster (Bristly Aster)

Ionactis linariifolius
(Aster linariifolius)   *Aster*

Violet rays surround yellow disks. Leaves stiff, numerous, ¾–1½ inches long. Stems stiff, growing in tussocks. Native.

Flower: ¾–1 inch.
Plant: 6–18 inches.
Blooming: August–October.
Habitat: Heathlands, dry fields, sandy or rocky soil.
Photo: Courtesy Arieh Tal.

Tall Blue Lettuce

Lactuca biennis   ***Aster***

Numerous small blue flower heads in large branching clusters. Leaves alternate, deeply lobed, coarsely toothed. Native.

Flower: ¼–½ inch.
Plant: 4–9 feet.
Blooming: July–October.
Habitat: Moist areas, damp thickets.
Photo: September 10, Eastham roadside.

Eastern Silvery Aster

Symphyotrichum concolor
(Aster concolor) **Aster**

Lilac flowers grow in long narrow racemes.
Plant nonbranching; leaves small, alternate,
both sides silky-hairy. Listed as Endangered
on the "Massachusetts List of Endangered,
Threatened and Special Concern Species,"
but is easily found on Nantucket and
Martha's Vineyard. Native.

Flower: 1 inch. **Plant:** 1–3 feet.
Blooming: September–October.
Habitat: Coastal sandy soils.
Photo: Courtesy Mario J. DiGregorio.

New England Aster

Symphyotrichum novae-angliae
(Aster novae-angliae)   *Aster*

Showy purple rays with bright yellow
disk. Stem stout, bristly-hairy; leaves
heartshaped, entire, crowded on stem,
lower leaves clasping. Native.
Flower: 1–1½ inch.
Plant: 3–7 feet.
Blooming: August–September.
Habitat: Meadows, thickets, damp areas.
Photo: September 22, Crane Wildlife
Management Area, Falmouth.

New York Aster

Symphyotrichum novi-belgii
(Aster novi-belgii)   *Aster*

Slender violet rays with yellow center.
Leaves narrow, pointed at end, slightly
clasping at stem, slightly toothed. Native.
Flower: 1–1½ inches.
Plant: 1–3 feet.
Blooming: August–October.
Habitat: Seashores and salt marshes.
Photo: September 14, John Wing Trail,
Cape Cod Museum of Natural History,
Brewster.

Late Purple Aster (Spreading Aster)

Symphyotrichum patens
(Aster patens)   *Aster*

Purple rays with yellow disk. Single
flowers at ends of thin stems. Stem rough,
slender, weak. Leaves short, pointed,
alternate, entire, clasping. Native.
Flower: 1 inch. **Plant:** 1–3 feet.
Blooming: August–October.
Habitat: Heathlands and dunes.
Photo: September 10, Wellfleet Bay
Wildlife Sanctuary, S. Wellfleet.

Wavy-Leaved Aster

Symphyotrichum undulatum
(Aster undulatus)   *Aster*

Pale lavender to bluish rays surround
yellow disk. Leaves wavy margined or
slightly toothed. Lower stem leaves larger,
enlarged at base and clasping stem. Native.
Flower: 1 inch. **Plant:** 1–3 feet.
Blooming: August–November.
Habitat: Open areas.
Photo: September 14, John Wing Trail,
Cape Cod Museum of Natural History,
Brewster.

Creeping Bellflower

Campanula rapunculoides ***Bellflower***

Striking deep blue 5-petaled bell-shaped flowers hang from one side of tall stiff stalk. Spreads by creeping and rerooting. Escaped from cultivated gardens. Europe.

Flower: 1–1½ inches.

Plant: 1–3 feet.

Blooming: July–September.

Habitat: Fields, roadsides, disturbed areas.

Photo: July 23, Cedar Tree Neck Sanctuary, Martha's Vineyard.

Sheep's Bit

Jasione Montana   *Bellflower*

Tiny cornflower blue flowers clustered
in small balls at tops of thin stems. One
flower cluster per stem. Basal rosette
of narrow pointed leaves. Recently
introduced to the area from Europe.

Flower: ½ inch.

Plant: 4–6 inches, trailing.

Blooming: July–August.

Habitat: Lawns and roadsides, especially
Highway 6 median.

Photo: July 10, Harwich Park & Ride lot
off Route 6.

Spotted Bladderwort

Utricularia purpurea   *Bladderwort*

Carnivorous plant with submerged root
system. Stalks rise straight up out of the
water, growing singularly or clustered.
Flowers two-lipped, with lower lip having
3 lobes. No leaves at flowering time.
Native.

Flower: ½ inch. **Plant:** 2–6 inches.
Blooming: July–September.
Habitat: Wet shores and bogs.
Photo: August 28, Ashumet Holly
Wildlife Sanctuary, W. Falmouth.

Viper's Bugloss (Blueweed)

Echium vulgare   *Borage*

Vibrant, bristly, outstanding. Bright blue
tubular flowers unfold one at a time along
one-sided short branches that line stiff
rough-hairy stalk. Long red stamens, few
clasping leaves. Europe.

Flower: 1–2½ inches.
Plant: 1–2½ feet.
Blooming: June–August.
Habitat: Roadsides, open areas.
Photo: June 12, Wellfleet roadside.

True Forget-Me-Not

Myosotis scorpioides   *Borage*

Beautiful sky blue flowers with 5 petals
and golden eyes. Flowers grow on ends
of branches that uncurl as blooms mature.
Leaves alternate, narrow, downy, one main
vein. Stems hairy. Europe.

Flower: ¼–½ inch.
Plant: 6–20 inches.
Blooming: May–September.
Habitat: Brooksides, wet places.
Photo: July 10, Wellfleet Bay Wildlife
Sanctuary, S. Wellfleet.

Blue Toadflax

Nuttallanthus canadensis
(Linaria canadensis)   *Figwort*

Tiny barely visible pale blue/violet flowers
on single slender stem. 2 white bulges
at flower center. Small narrow alternate
leaves on stem's lower half. Native.

Flower: ¼ inch.
Plant: 1–2 feet.
Blooming: June–August.
Habitat: Sandy or dry soil.
Photo: June 14, Wellfleet roadside.

Larger Blue Flag

Iris versicolor   *Iris*

Closely resembles the familiar garden iris.
Dark violet petals, white and yellow near
center. Several flowers per stalk. Swordlike
leaves. Often forms colonies. "Flag" is from
the middle English *flagge,* which means
"rush" or "reed." Similar to yellow flag
(page 26), but not invasive. Native.
Flower: 2–3 inches. **Plant:** 2–3 feet.
Blooming: June–July.
Habitat: Wet meadows, roadside ditches,
marshes.
Photo: June 13, Wellfleet roadside.

Stout Blue-Eyed Grass

Sisyrinchium angustifolium   *Iris*

Grasslike plant with one dark blue flower per nonbranching stem. Flowers have 6 distinctly pointed petals and yellow centers. Thin bladelike leaves rise from base. Native.

Flower: ½–¾ inches. **Plant:** 4–24 inches.

Blooming: May–June.

Habitat: Meadows, grassy places, damp areas.

Photo: June 24, Head of the Meadow bike path, N. Truro.

Sea Lavender
(Marsh Rosemary)

Limonium carolinianum
(L. nashei) **Leadwort**

Multibranching plant with tiny lavender
flowers at ends of many slender stems.
Basal lance-shaped leaves with long stalks
and prominent midrib. Leaves appear well
before flowers. Native.

Flower: Under ¼ inch. **Plant:** 1–3 feet.
Blooming: July–September.
Habitat: Salt marshes.
Photo: July 22, John Wing Trail, Cape Cod
Museum of Natural History, Brewster.

Water Lobelia

Lobelia dortmanna *Lobelia*

Pale violet (sometimes white) narrow tubular flowers spread out along tall stems. Basal leaves narrow, hollow, often submerged. Native.

Flower: ½–¾ inches.
Plant: 1–3 feet.
Blooming: July–September.
Habitat: Pond edges, usually in sand.
Photo: September 13, Gull Pond, Wellfleet.

Purple Loosestrife

Lythrum salicaria *Loosestrife*

Dense spikes of beautiful bright magenta
6-petaled flowers. Leaves opposite, lance
shaped, somewhat clasping at stem, usually
in pairs or whorls of 3. Highly invasive
garden escapee from Eurasia. Often
grows in large stands, crowding out native
aquatics that feed fowl and other wildlife.
Flower: 1 inch. **Plant:** 2–4 feet.
Blooming: July–September.
Habitat: Roadsides, marshy areas.
Photo: August 6, Wellfleet Bay Wildlife
Sanctuary, S. Wellfleet.

Virginia Meadow Beauty

Rhexia virginica　　　*Melastome*

Purple flowers with 4 petals and 8
conspicuous yellow stamens. Leaves
opposite, stemless, finely toothed. Native.

Flower: 1–1½ inches.
Plant: 1–2 feet.
Blooming: July–September.
Habitat: Wet sand and peat.
Photo: August 27, Harwich conservation
land trails, West Reservoir, W. Harwich.

Purple Dead-Nettle

Lamium purpureum   *Mint*

Purple irregularly shaped flowers grow in whorls at leaf axils. Leaves opposite, broad, heart shaped, roundly toothed. Upper leaves shorter stemmed, purple tinged. Sprawling stem. Europe.

Flower: ½–1 inch. **Plant:** 6–12 inches.

Blooming: May–September.

Habitat: Common weed of moist waste places and disturbed areas.

Photo: May 21, Lowell Holly Reservation walking trails, Mashpee.

Self-Heal (Heal-All)

Prunella vulgaris   *Mint*

Compact clump of small lavender flowers, each with a "hood" and fringed lower yellow petal. Square stem. Low creeping plant. Widely used as a remedy for throat ailments. Common. Native.

Flower: ½ inch.
Plant: 3–12 inches.
Blooming: July–September.
Habitat: Roadsides, lawns, open woods.
Photo: July 23, Cedar Tree Neck Sanctuary, Martha's Vineyard.

Common Skullcap (Marsh Skullcap)

Scutellaria galericulata
(S. epilobiifolia)   *Mint*

Blue flowers with arching hooded upper lip and flaring lower lip. Flowers grow in pairs in leaf axils. Leaves opposite, toothed, stalkless. Native.

Flower: ½ inch. **Plant:** 1–3 feet.
Blooming: June–September.
Habitat: Wet areas, pond shores.
Photo: August 6, Wellfleet Bay Wildlife Sanctuary, S. Wellfleet.

Mad-Dog Skullcap

Scutellaria lateriflora **Mint**

Branching plant whose bell-shaped flowers grow in pairs on one side of branches. Leaves opposite, toothed; branches opposite; stems square. Native.

Flower: ½ inch.
Plant: 1–3 feet.
Blooming: July–September.
Habitat: Moist woods and thickets.
Photo: August 27, Harwich conservation land, West Reservoir, W. Harwich.

Germander (Wood-Sage)
Teucrium canadense   *Mint*

Purplish tube-shaped flowers, with
prominent lower lip and protruding
stamens, growing in spikes. Leaves
opposite, toothed, oval, pointed at both
ends. Native.

Flower: ½–¾ inches.
Plant: 1–3 feet.
Blooming: July–September.
Habitat: Moist or wet soil.
Photo: July 23, Long Point Wildlife
Refuge, Martha's Vineyard.

Blue Curls

Trichostema dichotomum   **Mint**

Blue irregularly shaped flowers, with long coiling blue-purple stamens. Flowers at ends of long stems. Leaves opposite, entire, tapered at both ends. Native.

Flower: ½–¾ inches.

Plant: 8–30 inches.

Blooming: August–October.

Habitat: Dry open soil.

Photo: September 11, Truro Center roadside.

Climbing Nightshade

Solanum dulcamara   *Nightshade*

Climbing vine with purple or violet
shooting star shaped flowers, with 5
recurved petals, growing in clusters at ends
of long stems. Leaves alternate, entire, in
3 leaflets; 1 large leaflet between 2 smaller
ones. Eurasia.

Flower: ½–1 inch.

Plant: Climbing up to 4 feet.

Blooming: June–August.

Habitat: Thickets, roadsides, waste places.

Photo: June 24, Wellfleet Bay Wildlife
Sanctuary, S. Wellfleet.

Beach-Pea

Lathyrus maritimus   ***Pea***

Vinelike plant with numerous purple-
variegated irregularly shaped flowers
suspended above the plant. Compound
leaves with 4–10 roundish leaflets and
central stem ending in tedril. Fruit
resembles a garden pea. Native.

Flower: 1 inch.
Plant: 12–18 inches.
Blooming: June–July.
Habitat: Dunes and salt marshes.
Photo: June 11, Province Lands Visitor
Center, Provincetown.

Violet Bush-Clover

Lespedeza violacea **Pea**

Typical pea-shaped lavender flowers on slender stems. Bushy plant with oval leaflets in 3s. Loose-flowering appearance. Native.

Flower: ½ inch.
Plant: 1–3 feet.
Blooming: July–August.
Habitat: Dry woods and clearings.
Photo: August 29, Four Ponds Conservation Area, Bourne.

Wild Blue Lupine

Lupinus perennis **Pea**

Erect spikes of deep blue flowers rise above narrow palmate leaves. Similar to the garden lupine, but smaller, more compact. Native.

Flower: ½–1 inch.
Plant: 8–24 inches.
Blooming: June.
Habitat: Sandy fields, roadsides, open areas.
Photo: June 11, Nickerson State Park roadside, Brewster.

Cow Vetch

Vicia cracca **Pea**

Climbing plant with many blue-violet flowers on one side of long stems. 8–12 pairs of small narrow leaves on separate stems ending in tendrils. Stems hairy. Often used as a cover crop. Europe.

Flower: ½ inch.
Plant: 2–3 feet.
Blooming: May–August.
Habitat: Fields, roadsides, meadows.
Photo: July 9, Harwich conservation land trails, West Reservoir, W. Harwich.

Virginia Spiderwort

Tradescantia virginiana   Spiderwort
Blue or purple flowers with 3 broad petals
and 3 smaller sepals growing in umbel-
like clusters. Leaves alternate, entire, long,
smooth, narrow. Native.
Flower: 1–1½ inches.
Plant: 8–32 inches high.
Blooming: June–July.
Habitat: Woods and meadows.
Photo: June 12, Province Lands Visitor
Center, Provincetown.

Thread-Leaved Sundew

Drosera filiformis   *Sundew*

Small insectivorous plant. Tiny flowers with
5 pale lavender petals. Leaves long, narrow,
covered with sticky reddish hairs that trap
insects. This is the most common of 3 Sundews
on Cape Cod. Round-leaved sundew *(D.
rotundifolia)* has tiny white flowers, basal rosette
of sticky round leaves; spatulate-leaved sundew
(D. intermedia) is similar to previous, but leaves
have long stems. Native.

Flower: ¼ inch. **Plant:** 3–6 feet.
Blooming: June–September.
Habitat: Bogs and pond shores.
Photo: Courtesy Mario J. DiGregorio.

Blue Vervain

Verbena hastate   *Vervain*

Small 5-petaled, tightly clustered flowers
form stiff pencil-like stalks. Leaves
opposite, toothed, long stemmed. Square-
grooved stem. Native.

Flower: ¼ inch.

Plant: 3–6 feet.

Blooming: July–August.

Habitat: Open areas, roadsides, shores.

Photo: July 10, Wellfleet Bay Wildlife
Sanctuary, S. Wellfleet.

Common Blue Violet

Viola papilionacea   *Violet*

Blue-purple flowers have white throats.
Side petals hairy on inside. Flowers and
leaves on separate stems. Leaves roundly
toothed, broad, heart shaped, on long
stems. Native.

Flower: 1 inch.
Plant: 3–5 inches.
Blooming: April–May.
Habitat: Open meadows, dry to moist
woods, lawns.
Photo: May 7, Beebe Woods, Falmouth.

Birdfoot Violet

Viola pedata *Violet*

Flat-faced lavender flowers have white throats and conspicuous orange stamens. Flowers and leaves on separate stems. Leaves palmately divided into 5 or more narrow irregular leaflets. Occasionally blooms again in the fall. Native.

Flower: 1 inch. **Plant:** 3–5 inches.

Blooming: April–June.

Habitat: Dry open areas, fields, woods.

Photo: May 21, Shawme-Crowell State Forest walking trails, Sandwich.

Arrow-Leaved Violet
Viola sagittata
(V. fimbriatula) *Violet*

Lavender flowers have white veiny throats.
Mildly hairy flower, leaves, and stems.
Leaves long stemmed, oval (not heart
shaped like most violets), wavy edged to
slightly toothed. Flowers and leaves grow
on separate stems. Native.
Flower: ¾ inch. **Plant:** 4–6 inches.
Blooming: April–June.
Habitat: Dry woods and open areas.
Photo: May 22, Moraine Trails near
Goodwill Park, Falmouth.

Pickerelweed

Pontederia cordata   ***Water-hyacinth***

Aquatic plant whose small purple flowers form 3- to 4-inch clublike spikes. Leaves large, heart shaped. Roots submerged in water. Native.

Flower: ¼–½ inch.
Plant: 1–4 feet.
Blooming: July–September.
Habitat: Quiet ponds, streams, shores, wetlands.
Photo: July 9, Harwich conservation land trails, West Reservoir, W. Harwich.

Brown Knapweed

Centaurea jacea   *Aster*

Pinkish purple flowers in thistlelike heads.
Flowers at ends of numerous branches.
Leaves alternate, narrow, smooth. Europe.
Flower: 1–1½ inches.
Plant: 1–3 feet
Blooming: June–September.
Habitat: Roadsides, fields.
Photo: July 9, Thompson's Field,
Harwich.

Rose Coreopsis (Pink Tickseed)

Coreopsis rosea **Aster**

6 or more recurved pink rays surround a
yellow disk. Rays have 3 notches on ends.
Leaves paired, linear, grasslike. Native.
Flower: ½–1 inch.
Plant: 6–24 inches.
Blooming: July–August.
Habitat: Damp, peaty pond shores.
Photo: August 7, Ashumet Holly Wildlife
Sanctuary, W. Falmouth.

Eastern Joe-Pye Weed

Eupatorium dubium   *Aster*

Loose clusters of tiny pinkish purple fuzzy flowers form nearly flat-topped heads, 4–7 inches across. Purple-spotted stem. Leaves in whorls of 4–7, toothed, stemmed, narrowing abruptly at base. Native.

Flower: ¼ inch (clusters 4–7 inches).
Plant: 2–5 feet.
Blooming: July–September.
Habitat: Wet thickets and meadows along the coast.
Photo: Stock photo.

New England Blazing-Star

Liatris scariosa (L. borealis)   *Aster*

Tall rod-shaped plants with magenta
flowers forming shaggy thistlelike heads.
Leaves linear, alternate, lowest leaves under
½ inch. Rare. Classified as Endangered on
the "Massachusetts List of Endangered,
Threatened, and Special Concern Species."
Native.

Flower: ½ inch. **Plant:** 2–5 feet.
Blooming: August–September.
Habitat: Dry open fields, heath barrens.
Photo: September 23, Crowe's Pasture,
East Dennis.

Saltmarsh Fleabane

Pluchea purpurascens *Aster*

Pink flower heads form flat terminal
clusters. Leaves alternate, oval, slightly
toothed. A distinctive plant of salt marshes.
Native.

Flower: ¼ inch.
Plant: 8–30 inches.
Blooming: August–September.
Habitat: Seashores, salt marshes.
Photo: September 14, John Wing Trail,
Cape Cod Museum of Natural History,
Brewster.

Long-Bristled Smartweed

Polygonum caespitosum   Buckwheat
Spikelike clusters of tiny pink flowers with
5 petals. Stem jointed; leaves long, entire,
growing out of joints. Common weed of
gardens and waste places. Several varieties
with subtle differences grow on the Cape.
Asia.

Flower: Under ¼ inch.
Plant: 6–30 inches.
Blooming: June–October.
Habitat: Fields and disturbed areas.
Photo: September 14, Wellfleet
conservation land trails.

Seaside Gerardia
(Saltmarsh False Foxglove)

Agalinis maritima
(Gerardia maritima) **Figwort**

Pink to slightly purple tubular-shaped
slightly hairy flowers with 5 flaring petals.
Leaves opposite, entire, blunt, thick. Native.
Flower: ½–¾ inch.
Plant: 4–12 inches.
Blooming: July–September.
Habitat: Salt marshes.
Photo: Courtesy Jessie M. Harris.

Purple Gerardia

Agalinis purpurea
(Gerardia purpurea)   **Figwort**

Branching plant with many pink tubular
flowers on long paired stems. Leaves short,
narrow, opposite. Leaves and stems often
tinged with purple. Native.

Flower: 1 inch.
Plant: 1–3 feet.
Blooming: July–September.
Habitat: Moist sandy soil, meadows.
Photo: September 13, Gull Pond,
Wellfleet.

Plymouth Gentian

Sabatia kennedyana   *Gentian*

9–12 pink petals surround a yellow eye edged in red. Each plant bears up to 24 flowers. Thin stems; leaves opposite, entire, oval shaped, pointed at ends. Classified as Special Concern on the Massachusetts List of Endangered, Threatened, and Special Concern Species. Native.

Flower: 1½–2 inches. **Plant:** 2–3 feet.
Blooming: July–September.
Habitat: Wet meadows, pond shores.
Photo: August 7, Ashumet Holly Wildlife Sanctuary, W. Falmouth.

Stork's-Bill (Alfilaria)

Erodium cicutarium　　　*Geranium*

Small pink flowers with 5 petals grow in
long-stemmed umbels. Leaves pinnately
divided into small fernlike sections. Stems
and leaves softly downy. Considered a
weed by some. Mediterranean.

Flower: ¾ inch.
Plant: 3–10 inches.
Blooming: April–October.
Habitat: Sandy soils, disturbed areas.
Photo: Courtesy Jessie M. Harris.

Sheep Laurel
Kalmia angustifolia   *Heath*
Shrub with deep pink 5-petaled flowers
clustered near ends of stems. Leaves
opposite or in 3s, slightly leathery, paler
beneath. Native.
Flower: 1 inch.
Plant: 1–3 feet.
Blooming: June–July.
Habitat: Bogs, rocky to sandy woods,
dunes.
Photo: June 9, Lowell Holly Reservation
walking trails, Mashpee.

Small Cranberry

Vaccinium oxycoccos **Heath**

Tiny pink flowers with 4 recurved
petals, solitary or in end clusters on erect
stem. Leaves small, alternate, entire, with
slightly rolled edges. Shiny red berry.
Large cranberry *(V. macrocarpon)* is nearly
identical, but larger, and is the cranberry of
commerce. Native.

Flower: ½ inch. **Plant:** Trailing 4–8 inches.
Blooming: May–July.
Habitat: Natural and cultivated bogs.
Photo: June 13, Head of the Meadow
sand dunes, N. Truro.

187

Water-Willow
(Swamp Loosestrife)

Decodon verticillatus　　　*Loosestrife*

Aquatic shrub with magenta flowers
whose 5 petals grow in whorls where
leaves join stems. Leaves opposite, or in 3s,
lance shaped, smooth, bright green above,
pale and downy beneath. Native.
Flower: ½–1 inch. **Plant:** 3–9 feet.
Blooming: July–August.
Habitat: Shallow water.
Photo: August 6, Harwich conservation
land trails, West Reservoir, W. Harwich.

Swamp Rose-Mallow

Hibiscus moscheutos
(H. palustris)   *Mallow*

Large showy pink (sometimes white) flowers
with 5 wavy-edged petals, stamens united
in a central column. Leaves large, broad,
toothed, slightly lobed, long stemmed. Often
grows in large island stands. Native.
Flower: 4–7 inches. **Plant:** 4–7 feet.
Blooming: July–August.
Habitat: Seashores and salt marshes.
Photo: August 6, Harwich conservation
land trails, West Reservoir, W. Harwich.

Marsh St. Johnswort
Triadenum virginicum
(Hypericum virginicum)   *Mangosteen*
Pink flowers with 5 petals, long stamens,
protruding pistil. Leaves small, opposite,
stemless, rounded on both ends, obvious
center vein. Native.
Flower: ¾ inch.
Plant: 12–18 inches.
Blooming: July–August.
Habitat: Coastal bogs and swamps.
Photo: Courtesy Jessie M. Harris.

Blunt-Leaved Milkweed
(Clasping-Leaved Milkweed)

Asclepias amplexicaulis   *Milkweed*

5-petaled pinkish mauve flowers on long stems form loose round heads the size of baseballs. Several heads per plant. Leaves large, opposite, entire, wavy edged, downy. Stems and leaves ooze milky juice when crushed. A favorite of monarch butterflies. Native.

Flower: ½ inch (clusters 3–5 inches).
Plant: 3–5 feet.
Blooming: June–August.
Habitat: Roadsides, dry soil, open areas.
Photo: July 9, Thompson's Field, Harwich.

Motherwort

Leonurus cardiaca **Mint**

Pale pinkish lilac hairy flowers in whorls
where leaves join stem. Opposite leaf pairs
alternate at 90 degrees up the square stem.
Leaves have three points at ends. Europe.

Flower: ¼–½ inch.
Plant: 2–4 feet.
Blooming: July–August.
Habitat: Woods, roadsides, open areas.
Photo: July 10, Wellfleet Bay Wildlife
Sanctuary, S. Wellfleet.

Hyssop Hedge Nettle

Stachys hyssopifolia   ***Mint***

Irregularly shaped pale pink flowers
mottled with purple and white. Prominent
lower lip. Flowers grow in whorls in leaf
axils. Leaves narrow, entire, opposite. Erect
smooth stem. Native.

Flower: ½ inch.

Plant: 6–30 inches.

Blooming: July–September.

Habitat: Bogs, shores, wet areas.

Photo: August 7, Ashumet Holly Wildlife
Sanctuary, W. Falmouth.

Grass-Pink (Calopogon)
Calopogon tuberosis
(C. pulchellus)　　　　　*Orchid*

Several magenta pink flowers near tops of
slender stems. Each flower has one yellow-
tipped top petal, 5 other pink ones. A
separate bladelike leaf rises from the base.
Native.
Flower: 1–1 ½ inches. **Plant:** 6–16 inches.
Blooming: June–July.
Habitat: Bogs.
Photo: June 24, Head of the Meadow
sand dunes, N. Truro.

Lady's Slipper

Cypripedium acaule   *Orchid*

Deeply cleft pink pouch and 4 reddish brown twisted petals atop single stalk. 2 broad, smooth, clasping leaves grow from plant's base. Native.

Flower: 1½ to 2½ inches.

Plant: 6–15 inches.

Blooming: May–June.

Habitat: Pine woodlands.

Photo: May 23, Shawme-Crowell State Forest walking trails, Sandwich.

Rose Pogonia

Pogonia ophioglossoides   *Orchid*

Single dainty soft pink flower at end of
single slender stem. Flower's lower lip
fringed, yellow at center. 3 petals fan out
at back of flower head. One leaf midway
up stem, another at base. An uncommon
Cape flower. Native.

Flower: 1½ inches. **Plant:** 8–12 inches.
Blooming: June–July.
Habitat: Sphagnum bogs and fens.
Photo: June 24, Head of the Meadow
sand dunes, N. Truro.

Crown Vetch

Coronilla varia   *Pea*

Bicolored flowers form golf ball size
clusters at ends of stalks. Creeping plant
with small compound leaves. Makes a
lovely ground cover and is often planted
to restore nutrients, especially nitrogen, to
the soil and to prevent erosion. Europe.

Flower: 1½-inch clusters.
Plant: 1–2 feet.
Blooming: June–August.
Habitat: Roadsides.
Photo: June 24, Nauset Light, Eastham.

Everlasting Pea (Perennial Pea)

Lathyrus latifolius   *Pea*

Pink, sometimes purple, irregularly shaped flowers in long-stalked racemes. 2 lance-shaped leaflets; angular stems. Escaped from cultivation. Europe.

Flower: 1 inch.
Plant: Sprawling 3–4 feet.
Blooming: July–September.
Habitat: Roadsides, waste areas.
Photo: July 9, Cape Cod Rail Trail, Brewster.

Bristly Locust
(Rose Acacia)

Robinia hispida   *Pea*

Rose-purple (sometimes pale purple) pea-shaped flowers on short racemes. Leaves divided into 7–13 inch-long leaflets. Stiff, extremely bristly shrub. Native to Virginia and south, cultivated and escaped locally.
Flower: 1 inch. **Plant:** 2–9 feet.
Blooming: June–July.
Habitat: Dry sandy open areas, dunes.
Photo: June 10, Cape Cod National Seashore, Marconi Beach, Eastham.

Rabbit-Foot Clover

Trifolium arvense   *Pea*

Familiar and unmistakable fuzzy gray-pink
or gray-white flower heads, furry-soft as
a rabbit's foot. Leaflets in 3s, narrow, soft,
silky. Same with stems. Eurasia.

Flower: ½–1 inch.
Plant: 4–12 inches.
Blooming: June–September.
Habitat: Roadsides, open areas.
Photo: June 14, Indian Neck town beach,
Wellfleet.

Red Clover

Trifolium pretense   *Pea*

Erect plant with magenta to purple flowers on stalkless heads. Leaves in 3s. Used by farmers in crop rotation to restore nutrients, especially nitrogen, to the soil. Europe.

Flower: ½–1 inch.

Plant: 6–16 inches.

Blooming: June–October.

Habitat: Roadsides, fields, lawns.

Photo: June 25, the Knob, Falmouth.

Bouncing Bet (Soapwort)

Saponaria officinalis   *Pink*

Pale pink or lavender to whitish flowers.
5 petals, each having scalloped edges with
indent at tip. Petals tend to fold back.
Flowers form clusters up stiff stalk. Leaves
opposite, entire, oval, pointed at tips.
Common and abundant. Europe.
Flower: 1 inch. **Plant:** 1–3 feet.
Blooming: July–September.
Habitat: Roadsides and open areas.
Photo: July 10, Wellfleet Bay Wildlife
Sanctuary, S. Wellfleet.

Sea Milkwort

Glaux maritime   *Primrose*

Pink flowers, sometimes white or pale purple, with 5 sepals, petals absent. Leaves fleshy, opposite, entire, small, pointed at both ends. Native.

Flower: ½ inch.
Plant: 4–12 inches.
Blooming: June–August.
Habitat: Moist or dry saline soil.
Photo: Courtesy Jessie M. Harris.

Saltspray Rose (Rugosa Rose)

Rosa rugosa   *Rose*

Rose-colored flowers with 5 petals indented on ends and central cluster of yellow stamens. Leaves compound, 5–9 toothed opposite shiny leaflets. Stems mildly bristly-thorny. Common, abundant. Also grows with a white flower. Eurasia.
Flower: 2–4 inches. **Plant:** 3–8 feet.
Blooming: June–October.
Habitat: Dunes, roadsides.
Photo: June 10, Marconi Beach, Wellfleet.

Virginia Rose
Rosa virginiana   *Rose*

Showy pink flowers with 5 large petals, yellow center. Stems occasionally thorny; leaflets dark green and shining, coarsely toothed. Much smaller plant than saltspray rose (previous page). Native.

Flower: 2 inches.

Plant: 1–3 feet.

Blooming: June–July.

Habitat: Dry thickets and meadows, lawn edges, open areas, roadsides.

Photo: June 24, North Truro private yard.

Steeplebush (Hardhack)

Spiraea tomentosa   *Rose*

Tiny pink flowers with 5 petals in branching spikelike terminal clusters. Leaves numerous, alternate, toothed, white-woolly beneath. Native.

Flower: ¼ inch (spikes 2–4 inches).

Plant: 2–4 feet.

Blooming: July–September.

Habitat: Damp open places, old fields and pastures, swamps, streambanks.

Photo: August 7, Ashumet Holly Wildlife Sanctuary, W. Falmouth.

Lady's-Thumb

Polygonum persicaria   *Smartweed*

Tiny white or purplish flowers with
5 petals in dense spiky clusters. Stems
jointed. Leaves long, entire, usually with
a dark blotch in center. Common and
abundant garden weed. Europe.

Plant: 6–24 inches.

Flower: ¼ inch, spikes 2–3 inches.

Blooming: June–October.

Habitat: Disturbed areas, cultivated land.

Photo: August 28, Ashumet Holly
Wildlife Sanctuary, W. Falmouth.

Botanical Index

210

211